WHAT

AWESOME

LOOKS LIKE

WHAT
AWESOME
LOOKS LIKE

HOW TO EXCEL IN BUSINESS & LIFE

Amy Rees Anderson

ForbesBooks

Published by ForbesBooks, Charleston, South Carolina.
Member of Advantage Media Group.

ForbesBooks is a registered trademark, and the ForbesBooks colophon is a trademark of Forbes Media, LLC.

Printed in the United States of America.

10 9 8 7 6 5 4 3 2

ISBN: 978-1-946633-76-7
LCCN: 2018964871

Cover design by Megan Elger.
Layout design by Melanie Cloth.

This publication is designed to provide accurate and authoritative information in regard to the subject matter covered. It is sold with the understanding that the publisher is not engaged in rendering legal, accounting, or other professional services. If legal advice or other expert assistance is required, the services of a competent professional person should be sought.

Advantage Media Group is proud to be a part of the Tree Neutral® program. Tree Neutral offsets the number of trees consumed in the production and printing of this book by taking proactive steps such as planting trees in direct proportion to the number of trees used to print books. To learn more about Tree Neutral, please visit **www.treeneutral.com**.

Since 1917, the Forbes mission has remained constant. Global Champions of Entrepreneurial Capitalism. ForbesBooks exists to further that aim by bringing the Stories, Passion, and Knowledge of top thought leaders to the forefront. ForbesBooks brings you The Best in Business. To be considered for publication, please visit **www.forbesbooks.com**.

To Dalton and Ashley

TABLE OF CONTENTS

PART II: BECOMING AWESOME

PART III: LEADING THE RIGHT WAY

PART IV: STAND OUT AND STAY STANDING

PART V: FINDING FULFILLMENT

SO, WHAT DOES AWESOME LOOK LIKE?

I get it. You're busy. We're all busy. I mean, seriously, who even has time to read a book these days? I've got attention deficit disorder (ADD) myself, so if a book doesn't have big print and pictures I am typically out unless there is a genuinely compelling argument why I should be in ... so here goes:

I am an ordinary person who was able to accomplish something extraordinary. I became an entrepreneur when I started my very first tech company at age twenty-three, and, at forty, as founder and CEO, I sold MediConnect Global Inc. for over $377 million cash. BOOYAH!

How did I do it? The answers to that question might surprise you. They aren't the answers they typically teach in college courses, but that would make sense since I dropped out of college—not because I didn't value education; I just couldn't afford to finish back then—however, I did go on to receive an honorary PhD, so feel free to call me "Dr. Amy," since my family refuses to (at least not with a straight face).

Early on, I learned most things the hard way—trying, failing, learning from my mistakes, and trying again with the wisdom I'd gained. I went from bouncing so many checks at age seventeen they had to fly my father in to meet with the bank's president, sinking a ski boat, spending hundreds of dollars on a snow shovel, and typing clients' data into the computer manually because I didn't know data could be transferred electronically—to having an investor hand me a check for a million dollars based on my word alone, leading the development of complex web-based software systems, raising two children as a single mom and sole financial supporter, selling a company for $377 million, launching an angel investment firm, founding a charity to promote entrepreneurship as a pathway to self-reliance, and accomplishing every goal I've ever glued to my Goal Posters.

Along that journey I learned invaluable lessons, but I realized that if I wanted those experiences to benefit others, I would have to share them. So as CEO I began writing a daily blog to my employees. Interestingly enough, the more I shared in a completely open, authentic way, the better our profit margin became.

After successfully selling the company, I continued writing my daily blog, now making it accessible to everyone in hopes of helping others excel even faster and easier than I did, which led to *Forbes* and the Huffington Post asking me to be a contributor to their sites, and eventually to ForbesBooks reaching out to me to write a book, and *voila* ... here we are!

It's lucky for you that I have ADD (yes, I take meds for it ... no shame), because it helps me cover a lot of ground quickly, get right to the point, and be ALL KINDS OF FUN! Obviously, I won't fit everything I've learned in this one book (especially if it's going to fit the big print and pictures), but I've included several simple, tangible things that taught me WHAT AWESOME LOOKS LIKE!

~Amy Rees Anderson

PART I

GET UP, DO SOMETHING, DO ANYTHING, JUST MAKE A START!

CHAPTER 1

GET UP

Don't Lose Hope. You Never Know What Tomorrow May Bring.

One of the first experiences that caused me to question if I ought to give up happened about three years into my first start-up. I had been reselling another company's software, but as my business grew, I'd become impatient that the company wasn't adding in the features I felt it needed to best serve my clients. So I approached the development company and proposed a deal—I would take on the development of their software for them (they would retain ownership of the source code) if they would pay me an agreed-upon price to cover my costs of hiring and running the development team for them. The company agreed, and we negotiated the terms of the deal. In anticipation of our scheduled contract signing, I began hiring the software development team so that I'd be prepared to hit the ground running.

The day before I was to fly out to their office to finalize our deal, I got word that the FBI had raided their offices and stopped their ability to move forward with any deals while an investigation related to a recent merger they'd undergone took place. It was clear there would be no signing of a contract or funding from them for this development team I had just hired, yet I was now two weeks away from needing to meet payroll for all these new employees. It appeared to be a hopeless situation, and I had no idea what to do. I'd spent three years growing that company from a ten-by-ten-foot room in my home to a nationwide reseller, and I had done it the hardest way—by bootstrapping the business, growing it profitably one sale at a time. I'd worked too hard to just give up now.

I pulled my employees together and sat everyone down in a circle and explained the situation. They looked down at the ground, and the room went quiet. After a long pause, one of them started nodding his head up and down and said, "Well—there's always failure." The room stayed quiet for a moment and then all of us started to laugh. This employee had pointed out the obvious ... failure is always an option, but why in the world would we go with that first? My mind began racing: What if we were to develop our own software program instead of developing and reselling someone else's? I had the programmers hired and I knew exactly how I'd design it, all the features I'd want to include, and if we developed it from scratch we could develop it for the web. All I'd have to do was raise $2 million, but I had no idea how to raise that kind of money. I stayed up all night that night googling "how to raise money." The search came back telling me I needed to write a business plan. Yeah ... I had no idea what that meant. The closest thing I'd ever done to writing a business plan was drawing a diagram on the back of a napkin for my uncle and my dad when I raised the initial $23,000 seed money I needed to launch my business and become a reseller. From that point forward, I'd grown my company from zero dollars of revenue to several million by making one sale at a time, then hiring the employees I needed to help me deliver on that sale, then making another sale, and so on. I'd never actually written a business plan before. So I googled "how to write a business plan." The search came back with a little software tool called Business Plan Pro that I could get that would ask me questions about my company and use my answers to write a business plan for me. So I downloaded that software, and by the next day I'd written my very first business plan. Next, I had to figure out what to do with it, so back to Google I went to search for how to find investors I could send my plan to. By that night, I'd sent the plan to just about any investor I could find contact info for. One investor let me know he was coming to Utah for an unrelated trip in a few days and was willing to meet. I was ecstatic right up until the point in our meeting when he asked me how soon I needed the money and I saw his expression when I replied, "By payroll next week."

Long story short, we got the funding, and we went on to develop our own software, which became the first internet-based practice management system for physicians.

Little did I know back then that there would be even tougher trials ahead that would lead me on a journey that included starting a much larger company, acquiring several other companies to roll into it, and growing it to a $377 million exit. My entrepreneurial journey was just getting started.

We can accomplish just about anything if we are willing to do what it takes to work for it and if we stay determined in our resolve. And when hard times come, as they most assuredly will, we must never allow ourselves to lose hope that the best is yet to come.

Success Will Come and Go, But Integrity Is Forever.

If I could teach only one value to live by, it would be this: success will come and go, but integrity is forever.

Integrity means doing the right thing at all times and in all circumstances, whether or not anyone is watching. It takes having the courage to do the right thing no matter what the consequences will be. Building a reputation of integrity takes years, but it takes only a second to lose, so never allow yourself to do anything that would damage your integrity.

We live in a world where integrity isn't talked about nearly enough. We live in a world where "the end justifies the means" has become an acceptable school of thought for far too many. Salespeople overpromise and under-deliver, all in the name of making their quota for the month. Applicants exaggerate in job interviews because they desperately need a job. CEOs overstate their projected earnings because they don't want the board of directors to replace them. Entrepreneurs overstate their pro formas because they want the highest valuation possible from an investor. Investors understate a company's value in order to negotiate a lower valuation in a deal. Customer service representatives cover up a mistake they made because they are afraid the client will leave them. Employees call in "sick" because they don't have any more paid time off when they actually just need to get their Christmas shopping done. The list could go on and on, and in each case the person committing the act of dishonesty told themselves they had a perfectly valid reason why the end result justified their lack of integrity.

It may seem like people can gain power quickly and easily if they are willing to cut corners and act without the constraints of morality. Dishonesty may provide instant gratification in the moment, but it will never

In each case the person committing the act of dishonesty told themselves they had a perfectly valid reason why the end result justified their lack of integrity.

last. I can think of several examples of people without integrity who are successful and who win without ever getting caught, which creates a false perception of the path to success that one should follow. Although each person in the examples above may have gained the result they wanted in the moment, unfortunately that momentary result comes at an incredibly high price with far-reaching consequences. That person has lost their ability to be trusted as a person of integrity, which is the most valuable quality anyone can have in their life. Profit in dollars or power is temporary, but profit in a network of people who trust you as a person of integrity is forever.

Every person who trusts you will spread the word of that trust to at least a few of their associates, and word of your character will spread like wildfire. The value of the trust others have in you is far beyond anything that can be measured. For entrepreneurs, it means investors that are willing to trust them with their money. For employees, it means a manager or a boss that is willing to trust them with additional responsibility and growth opportunities. For companies, it means customers that trust giving them more and more business. For you, it means having an army of people that are willing to go the extra mile to help you because they know that recommending you to others will never bring damage to their own reputation of integrity. Yes, the value of the trust others have in you goes beyond anything that can be measured, because it brings along with it limitless opportunities and endless possibilities.

Contrast that with the person who cannot be trusted as a person of integrity. Warren Buffett, chairman and CEO of Berkshire Hathaway, said it best: "In looking for people to hire, look for three qualities: integrity, intelligence, and energy. And if they don't have the first one, the other two will kill you." A person's dishonesty will eventually catch up to them. It may not be today, and it may not be for many years, but you can rest assured that at some point there will be a reckoning.

A word of advice to those who are striving for a reputation of integrity: Avoid those who are not trustworthy. Do not do business with them. Do not associate with them. Do not make excuses for them. Do not allow yourself to be enticed into believing that "while they may be dishonest with others, they would never be dishonest with me." If someone is dishonest in any aspect of their life, you can be guaranteed that they will be dishonest in many aspects of their life. You cannot dismiss even those little acts of dishonesty, such as the person who takes two newspapers from the stand when they paid for only one. After all, if a person cannot be trusted in the simplest matters of honesty, then how can they possibly be trusted to uphold lengthy and complex business contracts?

It is important to realize that others pay attention to those you have chosen to associate with, and they will inevitably judge your character by the character of your friends. Why is that? It is best explained by a quote my father often uses when he is reminding me to be careful of the company I am keeping: "When you lie down with dogs you get fleas." Inevitably we become more and more like the people we surround ourselves with day to day. If we surround ourselves with people who are dishonest and who are willing to cut corners to get ahead, then we'll surely find ourselves following a pattern of first enduring their behavior, then accepting their behavior, and finally adopting their behavior. If you want to build a reputation as a person of integrity, then surround yourself with people of integrity.

There is a plaque on the wall of my office that reads:

"Do what is right, let the consequence follow."[1]

It serves as a daily reminder that success will indeed come and go, but integrity is forever.

The Power of the Goal Poster

Anything you can vividly imagine, ardently desire, sincerely believe, powerfully pray for and enthusiastically act upon will inevitably come to pass.

—Frank Edward Barrett

---

1   Anonymous, "Do What Is Right," *The Psalms of Life* (Boston, 1857), SCRIPTURES Deuteronomy 6:17-18, Helaman 10:4-5, Hymn: Do What Is Right.

I still remember sitting down to make my first Goal Poster. Yes, a Goal Poster. It began with a bulletin board, a pair of scissors, and a glue stick. I took pictures from magazines and pasted them on a poster board. I will admit that as I sat there cutting things out I flashed back to my elementary school days, but I refused to let my feelings of being childish stop me from completing the task of creating a visual picture board of things I wanted to accomplish in life.

The daunting part of this exercise wasn't the cutting and pasting, it was visually admitting the things I was secretly hoping to achieve. The thought of admitting these goals "out loud," so to speak, was terrifying, even if no one else were ever to see it. But I was going to force myself to answer the question, "What would I do if I knew I couldn't fail?" I included goals related to career, finances, spirituality, service, family, and leisure. I decided I wouldn't limit my goals to the circumstances I was surrounded with at that time; after all, I was raised to believe that the direction we are moving in life is more important than where we happen to be standing at that moment.

I included pictures of things like winning the Ernst & Young Entrepreneur of the Year Award, having my photo on the cover of a business magazine, meeting the CEO of Microsoft, the type of car and home I hoped to someday afford, and so on. Of course, I had no earthly idea of how I was going to make these things come about, but that didn't matter. This exercise wasn't about the "how," it was about the "what," and anything was fair game to add to my poster. I completed it and hung it on the wall of my home office just above my desk so that I could see it whenever I sat at my computer.

The years passed, and the Goal Poster became such a familiar presence that I hardly even noticed it was there. In fact, I don't remember focusing my attention on it again for the next ten years of my life. Consciously, I may not have been focused on it, but subconsciously there was no doubt that the Goal Poster was having an impact on me. How do I know that? Because years later as I was moving my office, I went to pull down my Goal Poster and realized that everything that was on that poster—literally everything—had been accomplished in my life. Every goal that I had set for myself had come to pass. I was stunned. That's when it hit me—I needed another Goal Poster, and this time it needed to include even bigger and better goals.

I sat down to create my second Goal Poster and this time I wasn't going to hold anything back—this time, I was going to shoot for the "amazing" and the "wow" of what I might accomplish. I included pictures representing me selling my company for a lot of money, starting a charity to empower others, becoming an angel investor, visiting the Seven Wonders of the World, and so on. I even added a picture of the Ghana Africa Temple that my father had given me when he and my mother left to go do service there. As they were leaving, he suggested I should have him perform my marriage in the Ghana Temple. To help paint the picture of just how lofty that goal was, I wasn't even dating anyone at the time. But I had faith in the power of the poster, and I wasn't going to waste its magic by dreaming small. This time I was going for the gusto.

I am happy to report that within a year of adding the Ghana Temple to my poster, I was out there getting married. So, to all the unbelievers out there, I say … what now?!?! The Goal Poster is clearly magic! But wait, there's more! Next, I sold my company for $377 million and launched the IPOP Foundation, a charity focused on empowering entrepreneurs. Oh, and I can't forget to mention that within a few years of making that poster, I'd already been to visit four of the Seven Wonders of the World. There were no doubts left in my mind that the simple act of creating a Goal Poster works.

I believe so strongly in the power of the Goal Poster that every time I publicly speak or teach at universities, I challenge my audience to create their own. I ask them to send me a digital image of their poster so that I can track them down later and see if they accomplished the goals they placed on their poster. To date, I have received countless images of people's Goal Posters from all around the world. Many have shared updates letting me know the ways they too have experienced the magic of the Goal Poster in their own lives. Their stories have proven to me that the magic of the Goal Poster isn't limited to me—it is available to everyone, everywhere.

I believe so strongly in the power of the Goal Poster that every time I publicly speak or teach at universities, I challenge my audience to create their own.

I continue to make Goal Posters to this day. In fact, writing this book was on my poster, so if you're reading this, it means another life goal has been accomplished. Yes, experience has proven to me that the only thing limiting me from what I achieve is the fact that I haven't cut out a picture and glued it to my Goal Poster yet.

I challenge you to make your own Goal Poster. Start by asking yourself the question, "What would I do if I knew I couldn't fail?" Just try it. My life is evidence of its power, and really, what do you have to lose? And if its magic turns out to be real, just think of what you could gain ... then go and glue it on your Goal Poster!

Success Follows the Incurable Optimist.

The greatest discovery of any generation is that human beings can alter their lives by altering their attitudes of mind.

—Albert Schweitzer

The most powerful personality traits to develop in one's quest for success are incurable optimism and integrity.

Optimism is defined as "the belief that good things will happen to you and that negative events are temporary setbacks to be overcome."[2] Integrity, as I would define it, is doing the right thing, at the right time, for the right reason—despite any consequence. When you combine those two qualities, what you have is a person who seeks out the best outcome in every situation, while still being honest and forthright about the facts of situations as they exist. A person who exemplifies these two qualities will garner significant trust and respect from clients, coworkers, managers, and subordinates—all of whom contribute toward helping that person achieve success.

---

2   Jane Brody, "A Richer Life by Seeing the Glass Half Full," *New York Times,* May 5, 2012, https://well.blogs.nytimes.com/2012/05/21/a-richer-life-by-seeing-the-glass-half-full/.

There is a Distinct Difference Between an Optimist and a Pessimist

An optimist sees challenges as temporary, able to be overcome, and as stepping stones that are leading them to a better solution. A pessimist sees challenges as permanent; they see them as massive stumbling blocks that make it impossible to move forward, thus signifying the end of that road. Finally, there is an *incurable* optimist, which is that optimist who relentlessly pushes forward, time and time again, never letting trials keep them from believing in the good that lies up ahead. These are the best optimists of all.

A good example of an incurable optimist can be seen in a personal story: When my daughter Ashley was a teenager, she passionately loved basketball. She worked incredibly hard to make the varsity team her junior year in high school, only to tear her ACL in the second game of the season. It was devastating news, but she was determined to have the surgery and be vigilant with her physical therapy so that she could be back on the court in time for the start of her senior year. She saw her injury as a temporary hurdle that hard work would help her to overcome. And it did—until two weeks before senior year was to begin, when she stepped onto a basketball court for the first time only to have her ACL re-tear as she drove to the basket. When the doctor confirmed she would need to repair her ACL for the second time, she realized her dream of continuing basketball had come to an end. Once again, devastating news to accept, yet within hours of her injury she began talking about the fact that there must be other talents she was supposed to discover within herself beyond basketball. That exemplifies incurable optimism at its finest. She recognized the gravity of her injury, yet she saw it as a temporary challenge that would lead her to discover additional talents and opportunities ahead.

Without question, optimistic people are a lot more fun to be around. They are genuinely happier, healthier, more attractive people. They have an energetic sparkle that draws everyone to them. I call this the "Tigger factor." If you think back to your childhood days of *Winnie the Pooh* and his friends Tigger and Eeyore—ask yourself who you would rather spend time around—Tigger or Eeyore? Clearly the answer is Tigger! Tigger is cheerful and happy and fun, a party unto himself, whereas Eeyore is depressed, grouchy, and just plain whiny. There is nothing enjoyable in being around a negative person. We are drawn to those people who display the Tigger factor, because optimistic people make everything happier. And let's face it—Tigger had the bouncebackability factor down. He was full of energy, courage, love, optimism, and faith that everything would work out fabulously simply by bouncing back.

> *Life isn't about how fast you run or how high you climb but how well you bounce.*
>
> —*Vivian Komori*

That optimism is of tremendous value for one seeking investors to fund their business. As an investor, I pay very close attention to the level of optimism of the entrepreneur seeking an investment. First, I'm going to have to spend time with that person if I invest in their company, and again, no one likes spending time with an Eeyore. Second, I need to believe that the entrepreneur I am investing in will be the type of person who can see a positive outcome for any difficulty they face. There will be numerous trials ahead in their business, without question, and I need that entrepreneur to use those trials as stepping stones to bigger and better outcomes rather than letting them become roadblocks to their success.

Optimism is of tremendous value for one seeking investors to fund their business. As an investor, I pay very close attention to the level of optimism of the entrepreneur seeking an investment.

It is important to point out that there is a huge difference between optimism and overconfidence. When someone is overconfident, they tend to ignore the barriers altogether, having an attitude of "That couldn't happen to me," whereas when someone is optimistic they have an attitude of "It may happen to me, but if it does I will find a way to get through it, and I will make it even better in the end." The attitude of the first person brings fear to the heart of an investor or an employer, while the attitude of the second gives a feeling of trust and comfort.

The ideal find for either an employer or an investor is that unique person who has both an incurable optimism and the integrity to share all the facts about things as they exist. They present the best picture without over-embellishing, and they express a positive outlook without overpromising. They can be trusted, relied upon, and to top it off, they are pleasant and fun to be around. With all of that, success is sure to follow them.

There may be only one Tigger in this world (and that one is fictional), but each of us can make the choice to become an incurable optimist and join him in the ranks of FUN, FUN, FUN, FUN, FUN!

You're Better Than You Think You Are

I AM … two of the most powerful words, for what you put after them shapes your reality.

—Gary Hensel

We've all experienced times when we've had a false sense of security, but we've also experienced times when we've had a false sense of insecurity—about ourselves. Too often, we are our own worst critics. When circumstances in life don't go the way we hoped, we often allow them to make us think less of ourselves, and we end up with a false sense of insecurity in our talents and abilities.

A few years into starting my first company, I began to notice a trend: whenever I was feeling insecure about my own abilities, everyone else working for me seemed to feel less secure in their abilities as well. A definite ripple effect would occur. I knew that in order for my company to succeed I needed my team to believe in

A few years into starting my first company, I began to notice a trend: whenever I was feeling insecure about my own abilities, everyone else working for me seemed to feel less secure in their abilities as well.

themselves, but it became clear that for this to happen I'd first have to become more secure myself. I set out to figure out how I could overcome my false sense of insecurity, and here are a few of the things I discovered:

- We cause a false sense of insecurity by focusing too much on how far we still have to go and all the challenges that lie ahead of us, leaving us feeling discouraged and questioning whether we're capable. To overcome this, we have to be willing to give ourselves credit for just how far we've come and how much we've already achieved. To do this, schedule time each week for a quiet moment—stepping away from the computer, setting to-do lists aside, and turning off the cell phones—to reflect on all of the trials we've already overcome, which then allows us to recognize just how capable we have already proven ourselves to be.

> **We cause a false sense of insecurity by focusing too much on how far we still have to go and all the challenges that lie ahead of us.**

- We start convincing ourselves that we won't be good enough until we have more than someone else does, or until we achieve something greater than they have. In our minds, we create an "us against them" atmosphere that makes it impossible to ever feel like we are enough, because inevitably there is always someone out there with more than us. By focusing solely on becoming a better person today than the person we were yesterday, we will be far more productive, and we will progress at a substantially faster pace. This also allows us to gain a better appreciation of what others are bringing to the table, because we no longer feel threatened by them. This allows our relationships with others to improve and naturally draws more people to us because they feel our genuine desire to see them succeed, and this then leads to an increase in our own feelings of self-worth and confidence. The more time we spend feeling happy for others, the less time we have to feel a false sense of insecurity in ourselves.

- Without a doubt, the best way I know to overcome a false sense of insecurity and feelings of inadequacy is simply to get to work. The more we engage in doing work that forwards a cause, the better we feel about ourselves and the more success we find. When Michelangelo finished work on his statue of an angel, he was asked how he produced something so beautiful. He replied, "I saw the angel in the marble and carved until I set him free." When we have a vision of where we want to go and we actually get to work at it, it is then that we will see our own masterpieces created.

Remember that the greatest successes don't always require the mind of a genius or huge sums of money. The greatest successes in this world are often achieved by very ordinary people who make a very extraordinary effort. Attitude, work ethic, and gratitude may seem like small and simple things, but when applied to your daily life they can make a huge impact on your level of success.

The people who become the most successful aren't the people who start with the most, they are the people who do the most with what they started with.

Redefine Failure.

Your journey has molded you for the greater good. It was exactly what it needed to be. Don't think you've lost time. It took each and every situation you have encountered to bring you to the now. And now is right on time.

—*Asha Tyson*

Fear of failure is said to be the greatest barrier to one's success, which makes total sense given that our fear of failure is what stops us from making attempts in the first place. Yet can anyone blame us for fearing failure? Just think about it: From the moment we are born we hear warnings to "be careful" and to "watch out," which relay the message to our young minds that the world is a dangerous place that we won't be able to handle. We are left with the distinct impression that if we were to attempt something new, we would likely fail—and that, based on the sternness of the warnings, failure would not be a good thing. Thus we begin to fear that failing will result in dire consequences to either our physical or emotional well-being. It may even make us unlovable. And so we are raised from a young age to live in absolute fear of failure. How can we move past that?

What we can do is redefine the meaning of failure. Failure isn't trying and not getting our desired outcome; failure is allowing our fears to stop us from doing the things we truly want to do.

Early on in my career, things I perceived to be failures at the time ended up being the very things that led me to my greatest successes. Each time I experienced failure, it ended up leading me in a different direction that became far more successful than I could have ever imagined. In my earlier years, when I'd fail and have no idea what lay ahead of

Failure isn't trying and not getting our desired outcome; failure is allowing our fears to stop us from doing the things we truly want to do.

me, I'd grieve and mourn as if it were the end of everything. Then I came across a story that helped change my perspective.

The story was about a man who was the sole survivor of a shipwreck, stranded on a small desert island with only the items from his ship that had washed up on the shore with him. The man carefully constructed a small hut to store his few precious belongings and to protect himself from the weather. One day, as he was standing in the ocean fishing for his next meal, he turned back to shore to see that his hut was on fire, with smoke billowing into the air. The worst was happening. "God, how could you do this to me," he cried. He believed that all was lost. Later he heard the sound of an approaching ship in the distance. It was coming to rescue him. "How did you know I was here?" asked the man of his rescuers. "We saw your smoke signal," they replied.

Destiny is a mysterious thing, sometimes enfolding a miracle in a leaky basket of catastrophe.

—Francisco Goldman

When things in life go wrong, we often fall apart, stress out, or get depressed and sad—yet in those moments if we could step back and consider that maybe, just maybe, the hard time we are going through is really just leading us somewhere far better and that what lies ahead is going to bring us success beyond measure—if we could just trust that God (or the universe, or whatever higher power you believe in) truly does have a grand design for our lives and that everything we are going through is meant to help us, prepare us, teach us, and lead us to a situation that will create the very best outcome possible for our lives—maybe then we would pass through those times more quickly and with less sadness.

Redefine failure. Trying, learning, and improving—that is the definition of success.

CHAPTER 2

DO SOMETHING

What Are You Passionate About?

---

*Do something, do anything, just make
a start.*

—Gregory Pearson

Whenever I speak at universities, one of my favorite questions to ask students is, "What career do you want to pursue or what business do you plan to begin?" After I hear their initial response, I like to ask, "Now, suppose I gave you a check for $10 million today and told you that you could pursue any career path or start any business you wanted to, with no expectation that you would ever pay me back or generate a return on my investment—and that I couldn't care less if the business never makes a dime. Now tell me what career you would pursue or what business you would want to begin." It is amazing how often their answers change to something completely different. Why is that?

Further discussion typically leads them to share the same conclusion: they are pursuing the path they believe will be the safest bet to a steady income, and in most cases that path does not include pursuing the career of their dreams or the idea that they are most passionate about. So then one has to consider if they are making the right choice. Does being passionate about the work you do increase your chance of success?

I can't say that there is an exact right or wrong answer to that question; I can only share my own thoughts about it, starting with a story about myself. I started working in health-care at the age of fifteen. At the time, I can't say that I took a job in health-care because I had a passion for it. Heck, I was only fifteen! All I was passionate about was being able to afford name-brand jeans.

As the years went by and my experience in health-care deepened, it was the obvious choice for me to launch my first company in that industry. I understood the industry, I felt confident about it, and I had the contacts and the network in that space. Was I passionate about it? I suppose I never stopped to ask myself that question at the time. By then, I was a mother with two small children I needed to support, and my greatest passion was being able to keep them fed and clothed with a roof over their heads.

As I began running my own company, I quickly discovered that I was also passionate about wanting to become a great leader and about being able to see problems and figure out ways to solve them by designing software that would simplify and streamline things. Note that none of these passions required industry specificity. The truth is, I could have fulfilled them in any industry, but with my past experience and knowledge, health-care technology became my industry of choice. And thank heavens that I did have passion, because when times got tough—which they always do in business— it was that passion that drove me and helped me persist through the worst of times. Had I not had passion, I honestly don't believe I could have led the growth of any company to a successful $377 million exit.

For some, their passion may be tied to a specific industry, like medicine, law, or science, but I tend to believe that, for most, their passion is tied to a desire—such as

Once you identify your passion, you can really begin to figure out what roads lie ahead that will allow you to pursue it.

to lead, or to teach, or to help others. And often these passions can be pursued in myriad jobs or industries.

What's important is to figure out is what passion will drive you to become the very best you can be. What makes you want to jump out of bed in the morning ready to take on the world? What will help you keep going when everything around you appears to be falling apart? What will make you want to give 110 percent of yourself rather than putting in the minimum requirement to pick up a paycheck? What is that passion for you? Once you identify your passion, you can really begin to figure out what roads lie ahead that will allow you to pursue it.

Interviews conducted with some of the most financially successful people of our time almost always contain a similar thread, which is that the key to their success involved following their passion.

- Warren Buffett stressed the importance of finding what brings meaning to your life and making it your focus each day.

- Steve Jobs of Apple said that people should do what they love doing. He shared that it was his passion for his work and a belief that "people with passion can change the world for the better" that drove him.

- Mark Zuckerberg of Facebook stated that people should find that thing they are most passionate about and pursue it. He said, "I think it's important if you're going to take on any big challenge, that you just love and really have faith in what you're doing."

So, going back to the question, "Does being passionate about the work you do increase your chance of success?" I believe the answer is yes. I believe passion gives you more energy, motivates you to work harder, inspires you to get more creative, drives you to search more diligently for solutions as difficult problems arise, and helps you inspire others working alongside you—all of which give you the greatest chance of achieving financial success.

There's No Such Thing as a Dumb Idea.

I often come across people who have a deep desire to be an entrepreneur and start their own business but who haven't done so yet because they "can't come up with a good idea." Too often, I hear,

"All of my ideas are dumb." And in those moments, I cannot help but say, "Define a dumb idea."

Let's take a look at a few things that one might consider a "dumb idea":

- Can you imagine sitting at the dinner table with your family and throwing out the idea to write a book called *Everyone Poops*? What a dumb idea, right? Yet this book has spent years sitting high on the Amazon bestsellers list. It even inspired additional great books, like *The Gas We Pass*. This "dumb idea" has been read by parents to their young children around the world—after paying good money to buy it. Dumb idea now?

- How about a blanket with sleeves? How dumb does that sound? Between the Slanket and the Snuggie, that "dumb idea" has ended up on bodies of couch potatoes everywhere to the tune of millions and millions of dollars.

- A mom has her two teenage boys take her pickup truck to do odd jobs hauling away trash from people's yards. The boys leave for college, but the phone still rings, so the mom hires two men to drive the pickup truck and voila, the next thing you know it's a company called … wait for it … Two Men and a Truck. Dumb idea? I don't know, according to founder Mary Ellen Sheets, in 2016 they did $442 million in sales! Cha-ching!

- Smash a stuffed animal until it's flat enough to be a pillow. Sound dumb? According to the Pillow Pets website, over thirty million units have been sold, generating hundreds of millions of dollars in sales.

- Marshmallows shot from a PVC pipe ... we've all done that as kids, but certainly it would make for a dumb business idea, right? Apparently not, as the company Marshmallow Fun has sold millions of dollars worth of shooters.

- Take a baby pacifier and glue on a fake mustache. One might say "dumb idea," except that I saw one at the store and I shelled out $15 cash to buy it for my friend who was expecting a baby. That's a "dumb idea" you can't help but spend your hard-earned money on, so how dumb is it?

- And one of my personal favorite "dumb" ideas: How about goggles for dogs? Genius, right? And we'll call them Doggles! Get it? What idea could be dumber than that? With millions of dollars in revenue, that dumb idea is being ridden all the way to the bank.

The point is that every idea has merit, because whether or not the idea sounds good, or is laid out perfectly, it can be worked and modified and morphed into absolute brilliance—even goggles for your dog.

In business, brilliant ideas are the ones that make money, not the ones that look the prettiest, sound the smartest, or are the most technologically advanced. The winners are the ideas that cause enough someones to pull out their wallet and lay down their money to pay for them. So who are you to judge how dumb your idea is until you put it out there to the world to see what the world is willing to pay for it. Every idea has elements of genius in embryo. Sure, it might need some tweaking along the way, but it will never grow to perfection if you stop it before it grows up.

Every idea has merit, because whether or not the idea sounds good, or is laid out perfectly, it can be worked and modified and morphed into absolute brilliance.

My advice is simple: Stop being so dang critical of your inner genius. You are restricting your "dumb" ideas from reaching their million-dollar potential! Try letting them flow for once. When an idea pops into your head, don't tell yourself that it's dumb. Rather, ask a bunch of people if they would pay money for that product you dreamed up this morning while eating your Wheaties. Don't be embarrassed to ask them. At best, they will tell you they love it or give you feedback on how to turn the idea into a product they would gladly pay for. At worst, they will say, "No, that's a dumb idea." To which you can simply respond, "Perhaps you wouldn't be so negative if you had a Snuggie and a Pillow Pet."

Recognizing Opportunities

I wish I would have thought of that!

Every day, we hear of amazing new business ideas that some enterprising entrepreneur stumbled on and find ourselves saying, "I wish I would have thought of that!" That comment is typically followed by a few moments of deep thought as we look in the deep recesses of our minds to see if the next great idea is lurking somewhere in there, only to come up with zip, nada, nothing.

So the question then becomes, "Where do amazing ideas come from, and how can I be the one to come up with one?"

One day in my early twenties I was working in a physician's office at the front desk, copying what seemed to be the millionth health insurance card from a patient. I had to make the copy so that I could then pull the patient's medical file, hole-punch the paper, and use the metal prongs to attach the copy to their chart, only to then go and file the chart back in its proper place. I thought to myself, "Why the heck can't I just scan the insurance card and have it attach to their patient registration information in the physician billing software we use in the office?" It seemed like such an easy solution to a very time-intensive (and frankly incredibly mundane) task that we were forced to do with every patient who walked through our doors. If I could just scan their card, I could save a huge amount of time in my day to use for other, more important, and far more exciting things. It seemed like a no-brainer to me.

So why didn't anyone offer that feature with their medical billing software systems? I spent months looking for a solution that could do this simple act of attaching a scanned image to a patient billing record, and came up empty.

So why didn't anyone offer that feature with their medical billing software systems? I spent months looking for a solution that could do this simple act of attaching a scanned image to a patient billing record, and came up empty. I thought to myself, "Someone should just write a new medical billing software program that has that feature. After all, how hard could that be?"

The truth is, it's a dang good thing I didn't know just how hard that would be, or I can pretty much guarantee I would have never started down the path of starting my own business at the age of twenty-three to make it happen. I started out completely unaware of just how difficult the path would be, and by the time I realized it, I was too far down the road to turn back. It was do or die, and frankly, I thought the "do" option sounded much nicer, so I went with that. :)

Each experience on that journey led me to the next one, and then the next one, and so on, and over twenty years later I thank my lucky stars that I was naïve enough to start down that path of entrepreneurship with my little idea. That journey has taught me more than I could have learned by any other method, and it brought countless amazing people into my life, each of whom have helped me become the person I am today.

I share my story because the idea that set me on the path to success was not earth shattering by any means. My initial concept came from being sick and tired of doing a task that was both necessary and ongoing, and I wanted to find an easier way to get it done. New technologies are coming out at a fast and furious pace these days, and the most successful business ideas often stem from simply applying a newer technology to an everyday annoyance in order to simplify a task.

If you want to come up with the next great business idea, start thinking about how you might simplify an annoying task that is both necessary and ongoing in your life. Focus on those tasks that a lot of other people out there are dealing with each day, because the more people who need an easier solution, the better. Each one of those people will become a potential customer for your awesome new solution. I personally believe that the lowest hanging fruit are the tasks that can be simplified by utilizing the latest technologies available that the competitors haven't yet taken advantage of. For big companies, incorporating new technology into your legacy systems is not quick or easy. As the little guy just starting out, you can be both quick and nimble, giving you a major advantage against the competition.

Face Your Fear—The Results Might Be Amazing.

Courage is not the absence of fear, but the mastery of it.

—*Victor Hugo*

Do you remember back when you were a kid? When you blew out the birthday candles to make a wish with the belief that it would actually come true? Or when you pinned a towel to your shoulders and played the superhero character that you just knew you would grow up to become? Or when you found joy in the simplest of activities, such as blowing bubbles through a wand? Do you ever look back and wonder what happened to that person?

We all came into this life with a positive view of the world. We were excited and imaginative, and we saw the entire universe as our playground. Then somewhere between college and middle age, many of us seem to lose that optimism for life. Perhaps this stems from telling ourselves that we have to "grow up" and become more realistic. Or perhaps it's caused by those doubts that creep into our heads, making us wonder if we are just not good enough to ever be that superhero. Or it could simply be the result of running ourselves ragged trying to meet the demands of those around us. Whatever the cause, we begin creating barriers and limitations for ourselves that cause us either to try, fail, and give up, or, even more prevalent, to fail to try at all.

I believe the biggest cause of losing our connection to that youthful excitement and optimism can be summed up with one word: fear. At some point we became afraid, and we let that fear stop us.

When I do public speaking about my entrepreneurial journey, I am often asked, "How did you overcome your fears? How did you stop being afraid?" The simple answer is that I didn't. I don't think I have ever stopped being afraid of things—but what I did was stop letting my fear stop me. I decided that it was okay for me to feel the fear—because frankly,

Once I decided that I was going to press forward in spite of my fears, it was like a huge stumbling block was suddenly removed from my path.

I couldn't stop myself from feeling it—but I was going to do whatever needed to be done anyway. Once I decided that I was going to press forward in spite of my fears, it was like a huge stumbling block was suddenly removed from my path.

I read a great book by Susan Jeffers in my early twenties called *Feel the Fear ... and Do It Anyway*. The book helps explain that having fear isn't something to be ashamed of, as everyone has fears. Rather, the book suggests that when we feel afraid we should think through the possible outcome that is causing our greatest fear and then realize that even if that outcome were to happen we would find a way to work through it. Sure, having to work through a negative outcome may not be easy or fun, but we will, in fact, find a way to move beyond it. By going through the exercise of dealing in our minds with the worst-case scenario, it allows us to mentally shift our thinking from "I can't handle it," to "I will get through it," thus allowing ourselves to move forward in spite of our fears. Another great trick I learned is to channel the childhood superhero I believed I could grow up to become—Wonder Woman. Whenever I feel afraid, I simply close my eyes for a moment, picture myself spinning around in circles and changing from Amy Rees Anderson into Wonder Woman. Then, as her, I go and do whatever it is that needs to get done. As silly as that might sound, you would be amazed at the courage that little trick has given me over the years.

You know, sometimes all you need is twenty seconds of insane courage. Just literally twenty seconds of just embarrassing bravery. And I promise you, something great will come of it.[3]

A famous quote states, "You are never too old to set another goal or to dream a new dream." It doesn't matter what stage you are in your life right now. It doesn't matter how young or how old you are. At any point in time, you can decide anytime to change your life to go after the things you really want. Would it be taking a risk? Perhaps. Anytime we take a step into the unknown, we are taking a risk. That's why it's called the unknown. So, what if you don't like the unknown once you get there? Then you will find a way to change it or move past it. You will. And what if the unknown turns out to be more amazing than you could have ever imagined it to be? Well, there's only one way to find out, isn't there?

---

3   Benjamin Mee, *We Bought a Zoo,* (New York: Weinstein Books, 2008).

Preparation Builds Confidence.

All great changes are preceded by chaos.

— Deepak Chopra

Whenever we have a major event coming up, whether it's a presentation for work, taking on a new responsibility, starting a new job, throwing a wedding, building a home, whatever it may be, the best way to build up your confidence is to prepare, prepare, prepare.

I am a self-proclaimed "preparation freak." When I'm planning something, I create incredibly elaborate spreadsheets that lay out every detail; I create Power-Points that give a visual of how everything is supposed to look; I make timelines for everyone

The best way to build up your confidence is to prepare, prepare, prepare.

involved; I have checklists for days. I do everything in my power to bring organization to insanity and chaos. Then, once I know I've done all I can do, I sit back, take a deep breath, and try to relax and enjoy being in the moment, taking everything in as it happens.

There is a confidence that comes with knowing you've done everything you can do to prepare, giving it 100 percent of your very best. And while there's no guarantee that everything is going to go perfectly just because you did your part, once you have done it, be willing to turn the rest over to God and leave it in His capable hands, trusting that everything will go as it should.

I'll be the first to admit that can be a difficult thing to do—I've had to go so far as to put a little note taped under my computer screen that says, "He's better at this than you are"—but the reality is, that's truly the only thing you can do. You can't control the outcomes, you can only control your efforts, so focus on those, and then sit back and breathe and try to enjoy the moment.

Ideas Are a Dime a Dozen. People Who Implement Them Are Priceless.

Ideas are a dime a dozen. People who implement them are priceless.

—Mary Kay Ash

The world is full of incredible ideas that never go anywhere because great ideas are useless without someone full of passion to implement them.

I realize that implementing an idea can be intimidating, but taking that first step forward is the most important thing you can do to get your idea off the ground. Analyzing an idea is an important pre-step, but one of the biggest stumbling blocks people face is the temptation to over-analyze in an attempt to solve for every potential problem they might face, even if it only has a .03 percent likelihood of happening. Recognize that in the beginning stage of your idea there is no possible way to predict exactly what the future will hold, because it is impossible to have every future fact you

Great ideas are useless without someone full of passion to implement them.

need to know. In the process of moving toward implementing your idea, variables around you will begin to change, and as they do, new facts will come to light that will help you pivot your ideas in the right direction. Go into it knowing that your idea is going to morph and change drastically before it reaches its true fulfillment. All great ideas do, and that is what you want.

Many years ago, I went to meet with several large customers to see how our products were performing for them. Each shared their satisfaction with our services but went on to share other problems they were facing, hoping that I might have a solution for them. As I met with each client and listened to their struggles, my mind began to formulate additions to our system design that were far broader in scope than my original ideas had been. The next thing I knew, voila, my original idea had morphed and become bigger and better

As I met with each client and listened to their struggles, my mind began to formulate additions to our system design that were far broader in scope than my original ideas had been.

than ever before. Had I not taken steps forward to implement my original idea, I would never have gotten to that moment when the original idea morphed into something genius!

As you get going, never be afraid to share your ideas with others to get feedback. As an angel investor, when I ask people what feedback they have gotten from their peers on their ideas, I often get the response, "I haven't shared it with them yet, because I am too afraid someone might steal my idea." My answer to that statement is always the same, "As an entrepreneur, I always felt that if someone else out there had the initiative to take my idea and get it implemented first, then more power to them!" The reality is that people may get excited about your idea, but very few of them would actually be willing to do all the work it would take to implement it.

Great ideas are born by the minute. At some point, you have to decide to stop talking about your ideas and take the first step with enough confidence to carry you through to the next step. With each step forward, new doors will open and your idea will expand. Keep your eyes and ears open, and never be afraid to share your idea with others to get feedback. Ideas grow best when they are exposed to a lot of other people's ideas and input on a regular basis. Never forget to stay passionate about your ideas. It's that passion that will carry you through the difficult times that inevitably come along the path of implementation. Your passion will be contagious, and it will draw others to you who can help you on your journey to becoming one of those priceless few who don't just talk about it, they DO IT!

CHAPTER 3

DO ANYTHING

Life Is Complicated Enough—Solutions Should Be Simple.

The most impactful lesson we learned as a software development company was that, in the world of software, less can be a whole heck of a lot more, and more can often lead to a heck of a lot less.

While serving as the CEO of our company, I became aware that our clients were dealing with a major problem. They had medical coders who needed to go through stacks of medical records and make annotations and highlights of important information that needed to be called out. These medical coders were printing massive numbers of records onto paper and then using yellow highlighting markers and ink pens to make the necessary notes. They would then take these marked-up records and mail them in boxes to central offices to be processed. The amount of paper being printed and mailed and the inefficiencies in the process were tremendous, and our clients needed a better solution.

As a software provider, we decided to develop a web-based system that would allow our clients to view the records in a secure online system that would allow the users to make electronic annotations, add electronic sticky notes, make colored highlights, and add countless markings to each record. This would eliminate the need for

The amount of paper being printed and mailed and the inefficiencies in the process were tremendous, and our clients needed a better solution.

paper and reduce the cost and inefficiencies they had struggled with previously. The user interface our team developed was spectacular. It had rows of icons along the top that allowed users to pick literally any marking color or pen type, change the thickness of their drawings, add countless different shapes and images electronically into the record, and numerous other bells and whistles that we thought would be fabulous to "wow" our customers with. The technical abilities of our completed system were simply fantastic, and we couldn't wait to roll it out to the customers so we could see their awe and amazement at the incredible system we had built.

Then came the rollout, and to our shock and horror, our clients were not using it. After trying it out once or twice, their users were opting to go back to printing out paper. How could this possibly be? Our beautiful, technically elegant product was not being used by the very people we had developed it for—where had we gone wrong? The product was powerful, the abilities were all there, and the options for settings were too many to count. So why were these users not leaping for joy over it?

Our next move was the smartest move we could have made—we asked our customers why they weren't using it. The answer was one of the greatest lessons a software company could ever learn.

The users were not using the product because it was simply too much—it did too many things, it had too many options. The number of options stressed the users out, and they simply chose to stop using the system. We tried explaining that they certainly didn't have to use any of the options available if they didn't want to—they could just ignore those icons on the screen and use only the ones they wanted. Their

Our next move was the smartest move we could have made—we asked our customers why they weren't using it. The answer was one of the greatest lessons a software company could ever learn.

response to that suggestion was loud and clear: "We don't want those options at all. We want them removed. We only want three buttons on the screen and we want them labeled with the words Highlight, Sticky Note, and Circle. Take all the other options away."

When I heard this, I thought, "How in the heck am I going to deliver this news to my developers?" After all their hard work to create such elegant features, I was going to have to tell them to strip their product down to the bare bones—down to something with three big buttons with words, not icons, as labels, indicating what that button would do. I knew the developers would see this as an insult to their technical genius and talent, and I dreaded having to ask them to make the changes to the system. But it was clear that short of making these changes to our beautiful, technically superior system, our software was going to be shelved completely.

So we did what had to be done and made the changes the users asked for. The bells and whistles were removed, and we reduced the options to three large buttons with the words Highlight, Sticky Note, and Circle. It nearly killed my developers to "dumb the system down," as they saw it, but they did what was asked of them, and once again we rolled this simplified, not quite as spectacular, software out to our clients.

The client response was amazing. Their users went nuts over it. They were thrilled at the changes. They absolutely loved it! The user adoption was immediate, and customer satisfaction hit an all-time high. Their users loved the simplicity. They loved the ease of use. They were no longer intimidated by the system, and training now took only a matter of minutes. This simple little system with its three big buttons became one of our most successful products.

So often we overcomplicate things. We assume that people want more when they really want less. The temptation to overdevelop and over-architect is constant, but it's important to remember that products only make money if users are willing to use them. It's not about the number of fancy features and killer options. It's about simplicity, ease of use, and creating efficiency.

Life is complicated enough. Solutions shouldn't be.

The Dos And Don'ts of Creativity

Creativity is seeing what everyone else has seen, and thinking what no one else has thought.

—*Albert Einstein*

Creativity—requiring a combination of innovation, inspiration, and a tremendous amount of hard work—is one of the most intrinsically rewarding endeavors we engage in. Creativity requires a combination of innovation, inspiration, and a tremendous amount of hard work. It allows us to explore both the wondrous potential and the incredible detail of things. And let's not forget that those little shots of dopamine that creativity releases in the rewards center of our brain … how could you not love that?!

Every single one of us has the ability to be creative. In the words of Steve Jobs, "Creativity is just connecting things. When you ask creative people how they did something, they feel a little guilty because they didn't really do it, they just saw something. It seemed obvious to them after a while. That's because they were able to connect experiences they've had and synthesize new things."

The Dos of Creativity

- Do be curious on a constant basis. Constantly ask "Why?" and, "Is this the best way to do it?" Recognize that others may do it a certain way just because that is the way it has always been done, not because it's the optimal way.

- Do believe you can do it. In order to accomplish anything great, you are going to have to believe that you can. In believing that you can, you open yourself up to the infinite source of inspiration that exists within each of us.

- Do your research. Coming up with creative ideas stems from understanding the problems or area of focus in depth. Gather data, ask questions, look at what has been done before, and look for ways to improve on it.

- Do get started. The number one most important element in creating anything is to start!

- Do stay humble and teachable. Ask others for their advice, opinions, and experience. Be willing to listen to and learn from the input of others. Then consider all that you learn and make the decisions that you personally feel best about.

- Do know that the best ideas don't have to be your own. It's your implementation of an idea that will lead to success, not the idea itself. Ideas are a dime a dozen, but the people who implement them are priceless.

- Do course-correct when necessary. The more you learn in the process of moving forward, the more you understand how to adjust your course to take you where you ultimately want to go. See course corrections as a positive element in your progress.

- Do persevere. It has never been a matter of being the smartest or the most talented; rather, it has always been a matter of moving forward, falling down, getting back up, and continuing to move forward a little wiser each time. Always keep moving forward. In the words of Steve Jobs, "I'm convinced that about half of what separates the successful entrepreneurs from the non-successful ones is perseverance."

The Don'ts of Creativity

- Don't be afraid to start. It is called the start for a reason … it is the beginning, not the end.

- Don't over-criticize your early ideas; doing so stops your creative juices from flowing.

To live a creative life, we must lose our fear of being wrong.

—Joseph Pearce

- Don't wait until you find the perfect idea to start. Whatever idea you start with will morph over time anyway as you continue to learn, so don't get hung up, just get going.

- Don't wait to figure out every little detail before you start. It would be impossible to think through every scenario and every possibility.

- Don't get discouraged when things don't go as you hoped. There are going to be a million failures before you achieve ultimate success—accept that it's all just part of the process.

- Don't ever do anything that would compromise your integrity. Success will come and go, but integrity is forever. Enough said.

Creativity is one of the most exciting and enjoyable parts of life. It motivates me better than anything else can. As Albert Einstein said, "Creativity is intelligence having fun." Not only is it fun, it's also highly contagious, so the more of us who get creative, the faster we can spread more fun!

Advice for Entrepreneurs Trying to Win Over Investors

I often get asked what advice I would give entrepreneurs who are trying to win over an investor. The most important advice I would give would be that when you meet with an investor, you have to learn to be optimistic in a uniquely realistic kind of way.

Being realistic is painful for entrepreneurs, because to them it feels like they are saying they don't believe in themselves or their idea. They tend to be constantly in "everything is going to be AWESOME" mode, especially when they are presenting to a potential investor. Herein lies the problem—that investor is about to take their own hard-earned money and gamble it on one thing and one thing only: trusting the entrepreneur.

> **When you meet with an investor, you have to learn to be optimistic in a uniquely realistic kind of way.**

Sure, the idea matters, as does market size, revenues, and costs, but more important than any of those factors is the person in charge. A fantastic leader with a poor concept will somehow find a way to make that endeavor a success, but a poor leader with a fantastic concept will almost always result in a failure. The investor is paying as much attention to the entrepreneur as an individual as they are to the idea; they are looking for an entrepreneur they can trust with their hard-earned money. Thus, the way an entrepreneur presents an idea will either inspire trust or destroy it.

Let's put this into perspective with a familiar scenario: Imagine a teenager taking his parents' car out for a drive by himself for the very first time. The teenager comes to his parents and says, "I've got this. No problem. Don't freak. It's all going to be fine." The parents' first reaction is: "Oh my goodness, he is going to total my car and end up dead or in jail."

Now let's try a different approach. The teenager comes to the parents and says, "I want you to know that I realize that driving a car is a huge responsibility and one that requires serious attention to my own driving as well as the driving of others around me. I know that despite my driver's education training, the fact is that there will be unforeseen circumstances that could arise during my trip, and while I don't expect anything bad to happen, I have thought through how I would handle any difficulties that could arise and I have tried to prepare myself with the proper emergency supplies so that I will be able to handle anything that may happen along the way. I also realize that you have a right to worry about me, and I will do what I can to communicate throughout the night so that you don't have to wonder whether or not I am okay and on schedule to arrive home safely."

The investor is paying as much attention to the entrepreneur as an individual as they are to the idea; they are looking for an entrepreneur they can trust with their hard-earned money.

Now, if there were a teenager who actually said that to his parents, I am quite certain the heavens would part and choirs of angels would be singing the "Hallelujah" chorus. But just imagine how good the parents would feel about trusting the teenager who approached it that way. Imagine the trust that would be inspired by knowing that while the teenager was optimistic that everything would be okay, they were also responsible enough to admit that life doesn't always go as planned and they were thinking through those "what ifs" in order to be properly prepared should the need arise.

Note that the action being contemplated was the same in both scenarios—the parents were handing their keys over to the teenager—but it was the teenager's approach to asking for those keys that made all the difference in inspiring the parents' trust.

So, entrepreneurs, as you prepare to meet with investors, remember to present your idea like the teenager in the second scenario. Go in with an optimistic attitude about your idea, but don't wait for the investor to start poking holes in your presentation with all the "what ifs." Instead, take the lead, and before they can ask, tell them about problems you've anticipated might arise. Help them see that you are putting careful consideration into all the possibilities of what could go wrong, and that you are prepared for them if they should occur.

So there you have it: the most important advice I can give is to be totally real and honest and upfront with investors. They are going to find out the truth at some point anyway, and it will go a long way to have that truth come from you. Don't fall into the insecurity trap—acting like you know everything, saying things like, "There isn't a competitor that can do what we do," or responding with, "That's easy … we aren't even worried about that." Remember, it's not a bad thing to admit the fears about the business

Be totally real and honest and upfront with investors. They are going to find out the truth at some point anyway.

that make you lose sleep at night. In fact, it can be the smartest thing you ever do, because many investors are looking for opportunities where they are able to contribute more than just money—they want to contribute the knowledge and experience they've gained and will often choose deals where those other contributions can have the greatest impact.

Trust the People with Experience: The Wovel Story

At the time my husband and I were married, I had been a divorced, single mother of two for many years, with a daughter who was eleven and a son who was fourteen. We were married on New Year's Eve, so winter weather was in full force, with plenty of snow coming down. During all my years as a single mom, I'd had fabulous neighbors who were always willing to shovel my driveway whenever there was snowfall, so I'd never had to deal with shoveling snow myself. It could be said that I was completely and totally inexperienced in the art of shoveling snow.

A few weeks after our honeymoon, there was a huge snowstorm. My husband came into our living room and said, "Babe, we need a snow shovel." I responded, "Why don't we just order a snow blower?" (All of our neighbors seemed to use them, so why wouldn't we?) He explained that a shovel would be better than a blower because we'd be able to teach our fourteen-year-old son the value of hard work and manual labor. He and my son then left the house to run some errands.

Being the independent and highly capable entrepreneur that I was—or at least that I considered myself to be—I decided to take it upon myself to find and purchase the most advanced snow shovel on the market. I googled "most advanced snow shovel" and was thrilled when my search results came back with a snow shovel that was recommended by Bob Villa himself. (I had been an avid fan of Tim Allen's television series *Home Improvement,* and I remembered that during their "Tool Time" spots they often sang the praises of Bob Villa as a tool expert.) I also found that this particular shovel had been named "Invention of the Year" by *Time* magazine, and even more importantly, it was touted as the world's safest shovel, and what mother wouldn't want her son to use the world's safest shovel to shovel her walks? It was clear to me that this shovel must be fantastic.

I wasn't deterred at the price tag of several hundred dollars, because I had never purchased a snow shovel before, so I had nothing else to compare it to. I even paid overnight shipping charges that were almost as hefty as the price of the shovel itself because the weight of the box was well over thirty pounds. After all, we needed it quickly in order to handle the snow that was fast accumulating outside.

Thrilled with my purchase, I waited impatiently for my husband and son to return home so that I could share the good news with them. When they arrived, I ran to exclaim the news of the amazing purchase I had just made for them.

"Why would you order a shovel online?" my husband asked. "We can just pick one up down the street from the hardware store." He was clearly bewildered. But this was no ordinary snow shovel, I explained. This was "The Wovel," the best snow shovel money could buy! Bob Villa himself endorsed it and *Time* magazine picked it as the "Invention of the Year." What could be better than that?!

I couldn't understand why he wasn't excited. When I explained that the shovel even came with its own instructional DVD on how to use it, he stopped the conversation and proclaimed, "Cancel the order." But I couldn't do that, as I had paid extra to overnight it and it was already on its way. I was caught off guard by his response—I thought I was doing something wonderful, and he was putting it down without even seeing it. Given that we were newlyweds and he didn't want to hurt his new wife's feelings, he agreed to wait until it arrived and try it at least once. Then if he didn't like it we would send it back. That was our compromise, but deep down I was certain that victory would be mine once he experienced how incredible my purchase was.

The next day, the box arrived, and when he saw that the shovel entailed a massive bicycle wheel and handlebars, he immediately refused to keep our agreement and insisted we box it back up without even assembling it. I reminded him that he promised to try it at least once. After making several comments under his breath about how no self-respecting man would be caught dead, etc., he proceeded to put it together. He then insisted that he was going to wait until dark to try it out so that there would be no chance of anyone seeing him. As he continued to grumble, my son stood in the background laughing uncontrollably.

My husband made it through a single line of snow before a car came driving down the road, and he literally ran into the garage to avoid being seen. By the time I came outside to bring him hot cocoa (being the good wife I am), he had disassembled the Wovel and was fighting with my son, who was hysterically laughing and insisting it not be sent back, as this was now a family heirloom that should forever hang in our garage. The next day, my husband drove to the local hardware store and bought himself and my son each a $10 snow shovel.

My husband grew up on a dairy farm in Idaho, and he has worked in all types of weather with all types of equipment. One could even label him an expert of sorts with all his experience in this area. I, on the other hand, have never shoveled snow in my life, and am in no way an expert on the matter. The lesson I took away from this experience was that we should trust the people with experience. Seek advice of those who have been there and done it firsthand, because no amount of research, studies, or endorsements can ever compare to someone who has actually been there and done it for themselves.

Seek advice of those who have been there and done it firsthand, because no amount of research, studies, or endorsements can ever compare to someone who has actually been there and done it for themselves.

Nothing Is More Expensive Than a Cheap Lawyer.

One of the biggest mistakes I made early on as an entrepreneur was hiring cheap lawyers or not using an expensive lawyer nearly enough, thinking I was saving money for my business. But over the years, the school of hard knocks taught me just how expensive cheap legal help can be.

I don't recall ever meeting anyone who enjoys writing a check to an attorney. Frankly, I can't recall meeting many people who like the idea of needing a lawyer in the first place. Heaven would be a world where the need for lawyers didn't even exist—where everyone could be trusted to uphold their word, no agreements would ever have misunderstood expectations, and a simple conversation could settle any dispute that arose. But we aren't in heaven—not yet, anyway—and we certainly aren't living in a perfect world, so the cold, hard truth is that when push comes to shove you better be hoping to heaven you have a great lawyer there to have your back.

Let's start with the importance of a contract. When I first started a business, I was embarrassed to even mention the word "contract." I thought that by even suggesting it I would morally offend the other party, causing them to think I didn't trust them. I wanted to be the person who took people at their word and believed that everyone had good intentions, and in my mind, asking for a contract went totally against that. It wasn't until one day during a call with my father, who happened to be a former FBI agent, that I first understood why my thinking had been incorrect.

When I shared with him my embarrassment about asking for contracts, he explained that the contract wasn't to say "I don't trust you." Rather, the contract was there to make sure I had laid out in writing exactly what my expectations and understanding of our agreement was, and to give the other person an opportunity to review those and make sure they expected and understood the exact same terms as I did. Putting it in writing, he explained, was about entering into a relationship with open and honest expectations from both sides up front, so that everyone was clear about what they understood from the get-go.

His explanation was like a lightbulb going off in my head. No longer did it seem like an offense to write up a clear contract with someone. Instead, it was a service to both parties to ensure that the relationship would produce a result that they could be happy with. From that point forward, I became a huge advocate of the importance of having a contract that was very clear and detailed, that laid out every expectation and left no room for interpretation or misunderstanding—not out of a lack of trust, but out of valuing and respecting the relationship with the other party.

Next came learning the importance of selecting a great lawyer. Early in my career, I thought that a good lawyer must be the scariest lawyer—a lawyer who would never back down and would fight like a gladiator on my behalf. WRONG! I cannot express enough how wrong that was. A fight-to-the-death, take-no-prisoners lawyer will alienate everyone you try to do a deal with; they will drain your pocketbook by dragging the fights out to the bitter end, and they will convince you that settling is not an option, because you are right and you shouldn't give in. In the end, a lawyer like that wins for one person and one person only—themselves. You, on the other hand, get to pay them for every hour they were able to convince you to let them keep fighting.

I finally came to learn, after many years of trial and error, what the definition of a truly great lawyer is: A truly great lawyer is one who will start the contract draft out fair and balanced, rather than trying to make a one-sided agreement with the hope that the other party will just sign without reading. A lawyer who is looking to take advantage of the other party is not the kind of lawyer you want, because business is about ongoing relationships, not churning and burning from one client to the next. A great lawyer is also one who will help you get a deal done. They will educate you on what terms you need to be more reasonable on as you negotiate with the other party, pointing out which points are truly important to keep in the agreement and which points are really not worth fighting over. A lawyer who will help you find a balanced win/win for both sides, while making sure that no one takes advantage of you, is the best kind of lawyer there is, and they are worth every dime you pay them, regardless of their hourly rate.

When I shared with him my embarrassment about asking for contracts, he explained that the contract wasn't to say "I don't trust you." Rather, the contract was there to make sure I had laid out in writing exactly what my expectations and understanding of our agreement was, and to give the other person an opportunity to review those and make sure they expected and understood the exact same terms as I did.

When I met Chip Lion with Morrison Foerster in San Francisco, he was representing one of my investors across the table from me in a negotiation. You heard me right; he was on the opposite side of the deal. But I was so impressed with the way he handled the negotiation of the terms during that deal that I turned around and hired him for myself the moment the deal was closed. That experience helped me realize that I only wanted attorneys working for me who knew how to negotiate a fair and balanced deal

A lawyer who is looking to take advantage of the other party is not the kind of lawyer you want.

where the two sides didn't have to hate each other when it was done, or where one party walked away feeling cheated while the other celebrated their win. Great attorneys are dedicated to facilitating a win/win. Did I still choke when I got a bill from Chip? Of course. But I never regretted paying it, because he was worth every dime.

I believe that a company should have multiple attorneys they work with, picking lawyers who specialize in each different area of practice. Law is so complex that no one attorney is going to be an expert on every matter. Some lawyers specialize in corporate law, others in tax law, and still others in litigation, or employment law, or what have you. Having lawyers from each specialty available to advise you is critical as you grow your business. And don't shy away from forming those relationships early on in your company. The more the lawyers can grow with your company, the easier it is to keep them in the loop on your needs and goals for the future.

The only regrets I have ever had when it came to legal bills and lawyers was either not spending enough money to hire the good ones, or the times I thought I was saving money by hiring the cheap ones. Go ahead and make as many jokes about lawyers as you want (because let's face it, some lawyer jokes are just plain hilarious!), but never forget that nothing will be more expensive to your company than hiring cheap lawyers, and nothing will be more painful than hiring the wrong ones.

CHAPTER 4

JUST MAKE A START

Unique Recruiting Strategies That Paid Off Big Time

Attracting the best and the brightest people to join your company is the goal of any good leadership team, but finding those people requires serious creativity in your recruiting efforts. Typically, the strongest talent out there is going to be gainfully employed somewhere else. So the challenge becomes finding the people who are not out looking for a job or out browsing the classifieds. Then, once you find them, how do you get them to apply with your company?

As the CEO of a company experiencing over 1,500 percent revenue growth, I found myself constantly dealing with these questions. I continually needed to find new people, and I needed them fast—but what I wanted most was to get the attention of employees who were currently employed elsewhere. To come up with a solution, I sat down with my team to brainstorm out-of-the-box ideas that we could use to get those people's attention. These brainstorming sessions resulted in amazing ideas that produced incredible results. Here are five of the most unique recruiting ideas that truly paid off.

1. **Fifteen-second wacky commercials**: People love going to movies. So we talked with one of the busiest theaters close by our headquarters and asked if we could buy fifteen-second spots to play some commercials right before the previews. We had to produce our commercials, but I didn't want to spend a lot of money on them, so I decided that rather than hiring a professional studio, I would reach out to my current employees and ask them to get involved. We asked employees to create their own six-second video at home of them performing their dumbest talent ever. We told them to be as silly and random as possible. Then I had my graphics person create an intro slide for the video that showed our company logo and then flashed the words "Featuring the Elite Talent of [Our Company Name]." We also created a closing slide that asked, "What Is Your Elite Talent? Apply now," with our recruiting web address displayed on screen. We then watched each of the employee submissions and chose the most entertaining videos and inserted each six-

second clip between our starting and ending slide to create our commercials.

We ended up with several commercials that were absolutely hilarious and entertaining but left people scratching their heads, thinking, "What the heck does that company do?" That curiosity then drove them to jump on their mobile devices and check out our recruiting website to read about our available positions. It was perfect!

Making the talents random was our way of encouraging all kinds of people to apply, regardless of their skill set and interests or abilities. One of the most popular commercials showed an operations manager balancing a toilet plunger upside down on his finger, then lifting his shirt and suctioning the plunger onto his belly and smiling at the camera. These totally random, silly talents did the trick, helping us find incredible new recruits that we likely would not have found otherwise. It was a perfect campaign, because the cost was low, the response was high, and it boosted employee morale by allowing them to be an integral part of the campaign. We hired a lot of great people from those commercials.

2. **Wrap an RV:** I mentioned before that we wanted to target new hires who already had a job. Additionally, there were certain companies we admired in our area that we felt were most likely to have a culture that would produce great people with good experience. To reach these people, we decided to take an old, inexpensive RV and have it wrapped—with the words "Now Hiring" in big letters—to create a mobile hiring center. We then drove the RV to the parking lots of these targeted companies and waited for lunchtime, when the maximum

number of employees would be coming and going. We had our employees stand at the RV handing out hiring flyers to people walking by. It was a fantastic way to do some targeted recruiting from great companies.

3. **Hand out recruiting cards:** We had special business-size cards printed for every employee in the company. These cards had the company name, phone number, and website printed on them with the words "Now Hiring" stamped across the front in red letters. We then had a place on the back that read "Tell them _____ said you are awesome!" We asked every employee in the company to keep these cards with them wherever they went. We told them that whenever they came across someone who was doing a great job at whatever job they were doing, they should give that person a hiring card and to write their own name on the blank line on the back. It didn't matter if it was a person in the drive-through window at McDonald's, the cashier at the shoe department in the mall, or the waitress who went the extra mile. We wanted to hire anyone who went out of their way to provide good service and who really made an impression. We'd learned long before that you can teach skills but you can't teach personality, so if someone had the right attitude, we were willing to teach them the skills. You would be amazed at the great employees we were able to find, from very diverse backgrounds, using this program.

> **These totally random, silly talents did the trick, helping us find incredible new recruits that we likely would not have found otherwise.**

4. **Employee referral rewards:** It is always better to hire someone who was referred by a current employee. A current employee

understands your company culture and can give a sense of whether a new person will be a good fit for the organization. To incentivize employees to refer others, we offered different items, such as cash rewards, free iPads, and so on, to employees who referred people that we ultimately hired. We staged their reward so

We'd learned long before that you can teach skills but you can't teach personality, so if someone had the right attitude, we were willing to teach them the skills.

that they received a smaller prize upon hiring and a bigger cash reward after the new employee had been onboard for a stated period of time. By staging it, we incentivized our employees to refer long-term hires rather than people who were only planning to stay with us a short time. Some of our more aggressive employees went to the extent of placing "Now Hiring" flyers with tear-off phone numbers on the inside door of bathroom stalls in office towers. Watching employees compete to find new, creative ways to recruit others was as rewarding as the recruiting results themselves.

5. **Billboards:** We found that renting billboards near busy freeway exits close to our location was a great way to let people know we were hiring. We made the imagery fun and catchy to draw people's attention. We also found that it was important to keep the wording to a minimum and to make the web address easy to remember so that once people were back at their computer they could look up the website and see the open positions. Our most successful billboard was one that had an employee posing in a company shirt with the wording "This is what awesome looks like ... Now Hiring."

Each of these ideas ended up being incredibly successful for my company, and each idea engaged current employees, which really helped to endear them to our business and increase their sense of company pride. The employees loved being a part of something that was creating so much buzz in the community, and they loved the excitement of building the business together. The payoff that came from using inexpensive, unique recruiting ideas was nothing short of fabulous, and I encourage you to expand on these creative ideas to help your own company.

Speed Dating Plus American Idol Equals a Brilliant Hiring Technique

You can't know enough in a one-hour interview. So, in the end, it's ultimately based on your gut. How do I feel about this person?

—Steve Jobs

As a CEO, I absolutely hated the job interview process. In fact, the entire hiring process seemed inherently flawed. We'd post a job description, and candidates would respond with a résumé tailored to the position described. When the candidate came in for their interview, we'd often sense a bad fit within the first few minutes, only to then feel obligated to continue the interview for the next thirty minutes out of courtesy and a desire not to be rude. When a candidate came in for the interview and passed that initial first impression, we found they tended to give the answers they thought we wanted to hear rather than engaging in a genuine interaction about their strengths. The entire process just felt flawed.

As the number of openings in the company multiplied, we realized that it was time for us to start thinking outside the box. A brainstorming session led to what could possibly be

As the number of openings in the company multiplied, we realized that it was time for us to start thinking outside the box.

considered a stroke of genius: What if we did "speed interviewing"— similar to speed dating, but without the need to buy anyone dinner?

What if we had candidates come in and do a two- or three-minute pitch about themselves? Realizing that we would need more than one executive to get a gut check on the candidate, we decided to structure our speed interviewing in the fashion of *American Idol*, with a panel of executives sitting on one side of the table and the candidate standing on the other, giving us their pitch. We didn't prep the candidate on what they should say during their limited time other than to suggest they express who they are and why they would be a good addition to our team.

Knowing that three minutes with someone wouldn't give us everything we needed to make an informed decision, we also set up a system that allowed us to do our homework on each candidate prior to their speed interview. To facilitate this, we

We decided to structure our speed interviewing in the fashion of American Idol, with a panel of executives sitting on one side of the table and the candidate standing on the other, giving us their pitch.

used the Wonderlic online testing system, where candidates would upload their resume, take an IQ test, and take a comprehensive personality evaluation prior to their interview. The executives would then be given copies of the thirty-eight-page personality analysis and the test scores, along with a résumé to review prior to each speed interviewing session. With these documents in hand, we were armed and ready to listen to their pitch. At that point, we took Steve Jobs's advice and went with our gut.

You Can Teach Them Skills, So Hire for Values.

The next thing we realized was that we needed to stop advertising specific job positions and start advertising for anyone with talent who fit the value profile of the type of employees we would hire—

It was incredible to see how successful the company became as it stopped targeting positions and started targeting talented people with values.

things like integrity, hard working, willingness to go the extra mile, and so forth. We learned that by posting specific positions, we were sometimes discouraging people who didn't feel they were the exact fit from applying while promoting a profile that candidates would tailor their skills to in order to appear to be the perfect fit. We changed our approach entirely and started asking people to apply to the company in general but allow us to determine the position their talents were best suited for. The results we saw by taking down the walls of the defined positions were phenomenal, and the talented individuals who ended up applying, regardless of their backgrounds, led us to hiring some amazing people who otherwise would never have set foot in an interview.

For instance, we hired a welder who ended up becoming a top account manager, a sprinkler installer who excelled as an IT tech, a mink farmer who thrived in sales, and people with finance and accounting backgrounds who were some of our best operations supervisors. The list goes on. Each of these individuals thrived in their position, yet none of them came in anticipating that those areas were the right fit for their natural talents. It was incredible to see how successful the company became as it stopped targeting positions and started targeting talented people with values.

We implemented this hiring approach, and as necessitated by our tremendous growth as a company, we held literally thousands of speed interviews. As we became better at recognizing talent, we were even able to shorten the initial interview from three minutes to sixty seconds. We would hold interviews each week, and we hired literally hundreds of great people at every level using this method. The time we invested in interviewing was incredibly small for the number of positions we were able to fill. The level of talent identified through this process was outstanding, putting to shame previous methods we had tried, and the retention rate of these new hires was equally fantastic.

I realize that our technique was completely out of the box and highly unusual, but I could not be more sincere when I say it was the most successful hiring technique I have ever witnessed in all my years as a CEO. Perhaps it was the fact that we tore down stereotypes of who should apply and for what position, or perhaps it was the comprehensive Wonderlic testing we performed in advance. Maybe giving candidates only a few minutes to talk brought out a more authentic view of each candidate's personality, or maybe the executive team, in seeing so many people each week for interviews, grew more trusting of their gut instincts on whom to hire. I can't pinpoint exactly what aspect of this approach led to our tremendous success in hiring the best talent; I can only tell you that it did.

Every Position in a Company Matters

There's no such thing as an insignificant position. Every single job in a company is of vast importance, and far too often people lack an appreciation or an understanding of just how impactful each position is in the overall success or failure of a business.

As CEO, I would often watch as employees across various departments would either feel that their position was the most important position in the entire company, or that their role simply didn't matter. Those who felt they were "better than" always thought their skill set or knowledge made them more critical to the success of the company than someone who performed a "lesser" job. Anytime employees felt this way, I knew it was time for an immediate intervention. I came to learn that this "better than" attitude almost always

I found that putting people through this additional training worked instant magic in giving them a greater appreciation for the importance of every other person in the organization.

stemmed from a complete lack of understanding of what went on in the positions that they deemed to be "lesser than." When these situations arose, I intervened by making every employee spend a few days or weeks working in the various departments of the company in order to have them experience each role firsthand. I found that putting people through this additional training worked instant magic in giving them a greater appreciation for the importance of every other person in the organization.

Prior to this intervention, these "better than" employees viewed themselves as the most critical component to our company's success, but they came away recognizing that without every department doing its part, none of us would be able to succeed. This exercise in mutual respect and appreciation was one of the most valuable exercises we put people through, and the results were tremendous. I highly recommend that every company implement this intervention for its existing staff, and include it as part of any new hire training programs.

So often in life, people can only appreciate what they have firsthand knowledge of. They only know how difficult their own job is, but a leader can help to rectify this just by exposing them to other jobs. Consider the following department-by-department rundown as it illustrates how connected each department in a company is, and the impact each department's successes or failures can have on an entire organization.

- **Marketing:** If marketing doesn't brand the company well and get its name out there, there won't be new sales coming into the business. If this department doesn't keep outbound communication flowing to the clients, there will be unhappy customers. Getting the messaging right to properly define the company is the marketing department's most vital role, and the entire company falters when marketing doesn't do it well.

- **Sales:** If sales doesn't follow up on leads, the company won't have new clients. If salespeople set unclear or unrealistic expectations for a client, the client will never be happy. If sales doesn't communicate the right information to a customer or to employees in other divisions of the company, the client will have billing problems, pricing issues, and complaints about delivery of their product or service. Thus, everyone in the company relies on sales to communicate accurately so that delivery can be a success.

- **Account managers:** If the account managers don't do a good job of training and supporting the customer and explaining the needed processes, the client will be unhappy and the company will lose the account. If account managers don't communicate new changes or requirements from their clients to other departments in the company in a timely manner, then those departments won't do their job correctly. If the account managers don't tell finance about client billing issues, then finance won't do their job correctly. If the account managers don't keep their clients happy, the sales team won't make additional sales.

- **Operations/production teams:** If the operations teams don't follow the proper instructions or training documents, they won't do their jobs correctly, the account managers will receive client complaints, and the sales team won't have good references to make new sales in the future. If the operations teams upset delivery partners, those delivery partners may not come through for them, leading to clients not getting their services.

- **Finance:** If mistakes are made on invoicing, payment application and posting, credits, and so on, clients will be furious, accounts will be lost, and sales will have no references. If finance doesn't make payments on time, delivery partners will get upset and services to clients will be impacted, which can result in losing business. If finance doesn't handle collections well, the result will be upset clients and the possible loss of business.

- **Human resources:** If HR makes mistakes, then payroll won't get issued, and we all know the stress that would cause in any company. If HR doesn't bring in good hires to the company, there will be a poor quality of employees, and every other person will be impacted because they are left to carry the extra burden. And if HR runs out of tissues, the entire company is in trouble! (Don't act like you have never cried to HR—we all have at some point.)

- **IT:** If the computers don't work or the servers go down, the company will have staff sitting and getting paid with no work getting done, which can cost the company a fortune. In addition, if the servers are down, the clients won't be able to place an order, which means no new revenue coming into the company, which means the company can't make payroll, etc.

- **Research and development:** If the applications crash, employees won't be able to work, the staff will sit getting paid with no production, and the company will lose money—or clients won't be able to place orders, and the company will lose revenue. R&D also has the burden of fixing help tickets and new system enhancements in a timely fashion, and any system mistakes they make can cause every link in the chain to fail.

- **Training and quality:** If training and quality don't do their part well, the employees will be trained poorly from the get-go, and everything, in every way, will fall completely apart. The impact of these jobs is clear and needs no further comment.

- **Front desk:** If the front desk person doesn't greet people with a smile, then people's impression of the company will be poor. If the phones aren't answered properly and politely and people aren't directed where they can get help, clients will be upset and the company will lose business.

- **Cleaning:** If the person who cleans the building and takes out the trash stops doing it, the company will have a really messy and disgusting office that is miserable to work in every day.

Every single person in a company is a valuable link in the chain. If anyone does their part wrong, the entire chain feels the effect. That chain is in a circle that goes round and round, with no beginning and no end. Every person matters and is equally important to the overall functions in a company. No one person is insignificant or small in the process. Everyone needs each other.

Employees should take their role in that chain seriously. Don't make mistakes that hurt others because you told yourself your job doesn't really matter or isn't that important. It is. And when you don't do it right, you hurt every other person and every customer you serve.

Don't ever think your role doesn't matter, because I can promise you that it does.

Remember Who You Are and What You Stand For.

All through my growing-up years, as I would run out the door of our home, my mother would yell, "Remember who you are and what you stand for." I would guess I heard that phrase literally thousands of times as a child. Most days, I would roll my eyes like a typical teenager, but now that I am an adult, I have come to truly appreciate the import of that one little phrase, "Remember who you are and what you stand for."

The following words are from a blog I wrote to my employees on my final day as their CEO. I wanted to leave them with the message I felt mattered most.

"Remember the values that made us the amazing company that we have become today:

- Integrity (honesty at all times and in all places—do what is right, let the consequence follow, no exceptions)

- Respect (to everyone, everywhere, without exception)

- Positive and optimistic attitude (be happy, be nice, and for heaven's sake, SMILE!)

- Dependable/trustworthy (do what you say, live what you believe)

- Flexible/adaptable to change (embrace the challenges, overcome your fears)

- Open to and implement feedback

- Going the extra mile (for coworkers, for clients, for shareholders)

- High performance/high production (give 100 percent every day)

- Knowledgeable (know the company, know the industry, know the client, know your importance to the success of the organization)

Don't ever forget that those values are what make you so successful. Those values are what make you better people—in your careers, in your family lives, and in society as a whole. Don't ever let yourself get sucked down into things that aren't right or would cause you to go against your values. Instead, you be the force that lifts all others up to where you stand today."

Looking back, I am so proud of what we accomplished as a team and as a company by living by those values. Living them brought not only professional success, but personal success as well.

If a person had to sell their soul in order to win, have they really won? My answer to that question is a resounding "NO!"

We live in a world that oftentimes appears to reward dishonesty, unfair practices, cutting corners, lying, cheating, stealing, frivolous lawsuits, and all manner of dirty tactics. It is discouraging to witness people using these tactics in their attempts to get ahead. It is even more discouraging to see those same people succeed in their quests. As disheartening as it may be, one must stop and ask the question, "What have they really gained?" If a person had to sell their soul in order to win, have they really won? My answer to that question is a resounding "NO!"

The more that people require integrity from their employers, their employees, their coworkers, their business associates, and the friends they surround themselves with, the less we allow for a world where those with a lack of integrity have the ability to get ahead.

I believe our greatest success in life is having the peace that comes when you "remember who you are and what you stand for" and live by it every day.

PART II

BECOMING AWESOME

CHAPTER 5

COMMUNICATION IS EVERYTHING!

Successful Communication: It Starts at the Beginning

Don't communicate to be understood; rather, communicate so as not to be misunderstood.

—*John Lund, EdD*

Years ago, I attended a seminar on communication by John Lund, EdD, in which he gave some amazing advice on how to better communicate with others. His input was simple and easy to follow, and yet very powerful. Here are some of the notes I took from his presentation.

How to Successfully Begin a Conversation in Business

Dr. Lund shared that men all the time and women (in business settings) want to know three things before they are willing to enter into a conversation with you:

1. Is what you want to talk about going to be painful?

2. How long is it going to take?

3. When you are done talking, what do you want from me?

If they don't know these three things up front, they will make excuses to avoid talking to you. Dr. Lund shared that your manager or boss will always want to know those three things before agreeing to a conversation as well. The reason he gave was that men and executive women always want to know the exit to the conversation before they feel safe engaging in it.

Men and executive women always want to know the exit to the conversation before they feel safe engaging in it.

So, for example, if you are calling a client, the very first thing you may want to say is: "I realize how busy you are, so I will only need one minute of your time to let you know about _____." This way, the other person knows it will be quick and painless and that you just want to give them a few facts on the call that will only last a minute. Now they can relax and listen to you as you share the requested information. Otherwise, without knowing if the call will be long and painful, they may try to make an excuse that they can't talk right now.

The same thing goes for a sales team. They call a prospective client, and the first thing out of their mouth needs to be something to the effect of "I realize that your time is very valuable, so I will only need two minutes to schedule a time for a second call where I can do a ten-minute demonstration of our _____."

The same advice applies when approaching your manager or boss to set up a meeting. Let them know if it will be painful, how long it will take, and the end result you are asking for—they will be much more apt to schedule a time for you.

How to Successfully Conduct a Conversation in Business

Dr. Lund shared some amazing tips on how to better understand the way we interpret communication from others. He also revealed some very interesting statistics on this topic. He said that when someone else communicates with us, the way we interpret their message is based on the following three things:

1. 55 percent is based on their facial expressions and their body language,

2. 37 percent is based on the tone of their voice, and

3. 8 percent is based on the words they say.

Dr. Lund said that these percentages are the averages across men and women together, but that if you looked at women alone, they would give even greater weight to facial expressions and body language and even less weight to the words. This tells us that it is critical that we become aware of what our body language is communicating to others as well as the tone we use. One thing I always recommend to people is to keep a small mirror by your office phone so that you can look in the mirror when you are on the phone, because it makes you more aware of the facial expressions you have, which makes you smile more, which in turn comes through in your tone of voice. It works wonders on how well you come off on a phone call, trust me!

Success in business is greatly impacted for better or worse by the way we communicate. Happiness in our personal lives is also highly dependent on this skill. If you don't believe me, just ask any married couple! Becoming a good communicator takes practice and consistent attention and effort, and it is a skill that we cannot afford to overlook.

Network, Make Eye Contact, Smile, and Say Hello.

Have you ever been in a situation where you feel like you don't know anyone in the room, or you feel like the odd person out in a situation, or you are simply the new person on the scene? I know I have. As a child, our family moved a lot—and I mean a LOT. While growing up, my family moved from Oregon to Washington, Washington to Michigan, to Virginia, to Tennessee, to Texas, to California, to Utah. I was constantly the new girl who knew no one. I still remember those feelings of being new and feeling like the odd one out. It was scary and intimidating every time we moved to a new location.

It wasn't until I became an adult and was just starting out in business that I discovered something incredible. I was at a business event where I literally knew no one in the room. I felt totally out of place and uncomfortable. In my head, everyone in the room was staring at me, thinking, "Who is this girl and why does she think she is welcome here?"

Then something amazing happened. A total stranger came up to me and smiled and put out their hand to shake mine and said hello. It was as if this person was an angel sent there to save me from my feelings of absolute awkwardness. The person sat and talked to me for a minute or two and then moved on to say hi to the next person. I thought, "Wow! That was awesome of that person!" I was unbelievably grateful.

And there it was—a light went on in my head and I realized one of the most important lessons of my life regarding networking: no one is ever going to be offended by having a stranger say hello to them. In fact, they will probably be grateful. Because nine times out of ten, everyone in the room is feeling just as awkward and uncomfortable as you. Everyone wants to feel accepted and acknowledged, just like you do—so why not be the one to walk up to strangers in the room, make eye contact, smile, and just say hello. You may just change their world, just as the person at that event changed mine.

No one is ever going to be offended by having a stranger say hello to them. In fact, they will probably be grateful.

From that day forward, I have been willing to walk up to people I don't know, look them in the eye, smile, and say hello. This new mantra has served me unbelievably well in my business life. It has opened doors and broken down walls and barriers in an instant. It has created bonds and friendships that have lasted for years.

All of us have an inherent need to belong, and all of us have the desire to be accepted and to feel included. Multiple studies have shown that the feelings of being included and accepted directly impact our psychological and physical health, and that mental and health problems are more common among people who lack social attachments.

For example, one study states: "Because social connections are fundamental to survival, researchers argue that humans evolved systems to detect the slightest cues of inclusion or exclusion. For example, simple eye contact is sufficient to convey inclusion. In contrast, withholding eye contact can signal exclusion .... Even though one person looks in the general direction of another, no eye contact is made, and the latter feels invisible."[4]

As part of the study, the authors measured how people feel when other people acknowledge them. To do this, they asked a college-age woman to walk around a college campus of about forty thousand students. She randomly selected around 280 people and made one of three gestures: (1) she looked through them without making any eye contact, (2) she acknowledged them with eye contact, or (3) she acknowledged them with eye contact and a smile.

---

4   Eric D. Wesselmann, Florencia D. Cardoso, Samantha Slater, and Kipling D. Williams, "To Be Looked at as Though Air: Civil Attention Matters," *Psychological Science* 23, no. 2 (February 2012): 166-168, http://journals.sagepub.com/stoken/rbtfl/Oe3XSfoYV/wsM/full.

Following a little ways behind this woman was another woman involved in the study. She would stop each person that the first woman had selected, and without letting them know she was affiliated with the first woman, she would ask them two questions: (1) "Within the last minute, how disconnected do you feel from others, on a scale of one to five?" and (2) "Within the last minute, have you experienced acknowledgment from a stranger, yes or no?"

The result of the survey is shown below:

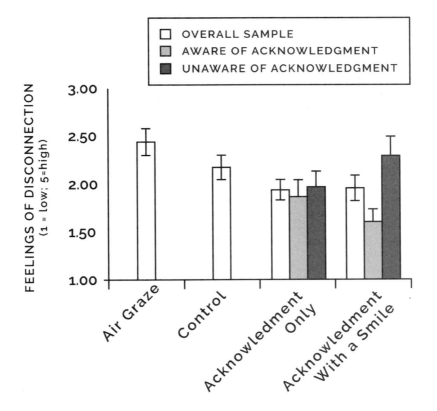

The people who got no eye contact felt the most disconnected. The people who got the eye contact with the smile felt the most connected—and isn't it interesting that over half of them didn't even realize the eye contact with the first girl had occurred when they answered the question. This little study suggests that our subconscious is picking up the positive acknowledgment received from others and that it contributes to our feelings of acceptance and well-being. Now that is powerful!

Here is my advice: Don't wait for others to acknowledge you. Go out and acknowledge others, and watch the impact it has in your life. Watch the impact it has on your career. Then watch the impact it has on you.

Keeping It Simple Doesn't Make You Stupid.

Genius is the ability to reduce the complicated to the simple.

—C.W. Ceram

I consider myself a somewhat intelligent person, but when someone explains a new concept to me in terms that are overly complex and unfamiliar, I struggle to easily grasp it. To learn a new concept, I need it described in such a way that I can relate it to something I am already familiar with. For example, when I was a young CEO starting a software company, I needed to learn about computer hardware so that I could speak intelligently about it. I asked my IT employees to teach me, and they proceeded to explain to me that computers were made up of a hard drive that stored gigabytes of data, random access memory (RAM), a central processing unit (CPU), and so on. They may as well have been speaking Chinese to me at that point, because although I could hear the words they were saying, I couldn't relate them to anything that was familiar to me. I left the room feeling discouraged and frustrated.

Desperate to understand computer hardware, I turned to my younger brother, who was revered as a genius on computers. I told him how lost I felt amid all the technical words being thrown at me, and I begged him to find a way to dumb it down into terms I could understand. What he described to me next was nothing short of amazing. He told me to pretend that the local library was the computer box itself. He explained that in the library were racks of shelves holding books and each of these racks represented gigabytes of hard drive storage. The more gigabytes of space, the more racks of books your computer shelves could hold. He explained that the table in the library where I sat to read my book was like the computer's RAM. The size of the table, or the amount of RAM, determined the number of open books I could have open on my table to view at one time. He shared that the computer's CPU was like my brain in the library directing my body to do tasks, such as getting a book off the shelf, opening the book, reading the book, etc. The more cores the CPU had, the more tasks (known as threads) I could perform simultaneously. He went on to describe the rest of the computer's hardware in this same fashion.

Everything he said made perfect sense. He had taken a very complicated subject and made it into the simplest. His ability to simplify the subject didn't make him less intelligent; it made him a genius!

That experience taught me that the best proof of someone's intelligence is their ability to simplify the complex. During my years as a CEO, I observed that people who are confident in their knowledge won't hesitate to share it with others in terms that are easily understood. Whereas, people who attempt to talk over people's heads through the use of overly complex terms and descriptions are typically those who lack a true understanding of the subject themselves and are trying to mask that fact.

> *If you can't explain it to a six year old, you don't understand it yourself.*
>
> —Albert Einstein

Too often, people overcomplicate things in business in an attempt to display their intelligence, when in reality they end up pushing people away and ultimately losing credibility. They come off as an elitist rather thana team player. Truly intelligent people are not afraid to share their knowledge, because they don't view other people gaining knowledge as a threat to their own. Rather, they take pleasure in sharing and teaching others. As a result, they become builders of people, and they contribute tremendously to a company's overall success.

One of the most common areas where complicating things kills a company is sales. Keeping the sales pitch simple and directly focused on how it will impact the customer's life for the better is the best way to make a sale. Salespeople in general tend to spend too much time focusing the conversation on their product or company rather than on how their product or service will directly benefit the customer. The moment they get too technical and complex is the moment they start to lose the sale. A perfect example of how to

Truly intelligent people are not afraid to share their knowledge, because they don't view other people gaining knowledge as a threat.

simplify a sale is the way Apple sells iPods. Rather than focusing on the number of gigabytes the iPod has, they focus on the number of songs it will hold, because that is a personal benefit that is simple for every potential customer to understand.

We've all heard the phrase "Keep it simple, stupid." The truth is that keeping it simple requires confidence and humility. Recognize that we don't have to talk like a super genius to be seen as intelligent. There is tremendous genius in our ability to keep it simple. Many of the world's most difficult problems have been solved with the simplest solutions.

Make Communication Accessible, Consistent, Bidirectional, and Inclusive.

As CEO of a high-growth company, I found it necessary to implement a few simple but incredibly powerful tools to help create an environment that encouraged the contribution and open sharing of information within the company. Truth be told, as these tools took hold throughout the company, they gradually gave life to an amazing corporate culture. This led to improvements in employee satisfaction, retention, and productivity, which quickly led to improvements in quality and customer satisfaction, which led to growth in revenues and profitability. As communication improved, culture improved, and so did the bottom line. Here are the four tools that made all the difference.

CEO Daily Message Board

I am a firm believer in the notion that leadership has to start at the top. If a CEO is unwilling to participate in the contribution and open sharing of information, then quite frankly, it just won't happen. As a leader, I felt the same burden that all leaders feel of having too

> **I came to realize that no matter what I had on my plate, nothing was going to be more important and impactful to the organization than the employees hearing directly from me each day.**

much on my plate and not enough hours in my day, so the thought of having to write a daily message to my employees seemed like an overwhelming and unachievable task. However, I came to realize that no matter what I had on my plate, nothing was going to be

more important and impactful to the organization than the employees hearing directly from me each day. Not because I was special or more important than anyone else in the company, because I wasn't, but because I was the CEO and there is a responsibility and a duty to communicate that comes with that title that leaders shouldn't shrink from. Our solution was to create an internal company home page that provided links to all of our company information for employees as well as shortcuts to all of our internal systems so that employees would need to start their day from this homepage each morning. Displayed front and center on this homepage was a CEO Daily Message for all employees to read. I wrote the messages myself each evening to post the following morning. Some messages were shorter and some were longer, but I posted every day, five days a week. The messages contained anything from important company-wide announcements, to a simple motivational thought, to concerns I had about the company, to mistakes I had made and the lessons I learned from them, to recognizing great performers, to sharing goals for our company, to reiterating our values. It didn't really matter how long the message was; what mattered was that they were consistent, that they were open, and that they were genuine and real. Employees don't want to hear formal messages from their boss; they want a boss who is real, and human, and fallible, and who cares. The more I shared, the more the employees got behind me and supported me as their leader, the quicker they forgave me when I made mistakes, and the more they cared about helping each other and the company succeed.

Employee Directory

One of the most daunting things for new employees joining an organization, especially a large one, is understanding where every other employee fits into the overall company structure and culture. An easy way to help facilitate this process is to have a robust online employee directory—but to make the directory truly valuable, it is necessary to give more detail than just a title, an email, and a phone extension. By adding information to each person's profile such as what responsibilities they handle (such as payroll matters, employee benefits, software questions, and so forth) and by including awards that person has received from the company and how long their tenure has been, you give other employees a better sense of who to reach out to on the matters they need assistance with. This can help eliminate bottlenecks and facilitate efficiency throughout the organization. In addition, by sharing a little about each person's personal interests and talents and hopes, you can truly begin creating a culture where people come to know and care about one another's future success.

Employee Discussion Board

One thing that I found incredibly helpful was the implementation of an online employee discussion board, where any employee could post questions or comments, and every other employee could respond. At first, I was a bit apprehensive as to whether this discussion board would turn into a breeding ground for negativity and complaining, but those fears could not have been more wrong. In fact, what I found was that as one employee would post a complaint about something, ten other employees would quickly post solutions and encouragement on how to resolve the concern. In essence, the employees themselves began resolving employee problems and

Prior to having this discussion board, the feelings of discontent would have simmered and spread for weeks or even months.

complaints on their own through these open discussions. Not only that, but as a management team, we were able to stay completely on top of the feelings and concerns of the employees on a real-time basis, which allowed us to better understand and more readily address their needs. This proved to be a tremendous value to our company, as prior to having this discussion board, the feelings of discontent would have simmered and spread for weeks or even months—becoming somewhat of a cancer in the organization before management even became aware of them. And as you'd imagine, resolving problems once they have spread becomes infinitely more difficult. Allowing open discussions proved to be helpful to the employees, the management team, and to me as the CEO. It was a huge morale boost for all of us to see all the positive reinforcement that employees would offer one another on this discussion board on a daily basis. It made everyone feel more involved and needed throughout our entire organization, and overall job satisfaction and employee retention improved drastically.

Company Idea Board

Sometimes we become so head down in our own jobs that creativity suffers and we have a hard time thinking out of the box. To overcome this problem, we decided to implement an online idea board, a place where anyone in the company could post any idea they had about how we could make the company better. It could be a software development improvement, a policy change, a customer service offering, a payroll process change, or literally any idea they felt would make us a better company. As each employee posted their ideas, every other employee could go online and vote for it if they liked it, much like clicking "Like" on a Facebook or Instagram post. The idea list would grow daily, and employees would vote when they felt an idea had merit. Once a week, the executive team would meet and review the top-voted ideas currently on the idea board and determine which to implement.

The amount of creativity and innovation that came from these ideas being posted was incredible. And the most surprising thing was that many of the very best ideas came from people whose current job duties had nothing to do with the problem they had an idea about— for example, a receptionist suggested an amazing idea for streamlining a payment posting process for the finance department, a mailroom employee suggested a programming change that improved customer service, and an operations employee came up with an incredible new marketing campaign. The ideas for improvement came from people all through the company, on every aspect of the business. The idea gathering from every employee regarding every facet of the company, without constraining people to think only of improvements in their own areas, changed our entire company into a massive engine for innovation and creative ideas. And I cannot begin to express how rewarding it is to witness employees' self-confidence rising as they receive recognition for contributing ideas that really make a difference. The ownership that employees begin to feel over the company's success is something even money can't buy.

CHAPTER 6

HAPPINESS IS A CHOICE

Stop the Negative Self-Talk.

Never say anything about yourself that you don't want to come true.

—Brian Tracy

I still remember, as a child, seeing my mother standing in the kitchen talking to herself. No joke—she would literally have entire conversations with herself. At the time, I just assumed my mom must be a little bit crazy; after all, the woman had ten children, so by right she was entitled to be at least somewhat nuts. Then I grew up and became an adult myself and realized that those conversations she had with herself didn't mean she was crazy at all. In fact, they were a stroke of genius, and probably the only way she kept her sanity while raising those ten kids (or I would argue nine, since I was an angel child).

When I became the CEO of my first company, I found myself having all kinds of conversations with myself, only I found it was far less suspect to have them inside my head rather than out loud, because let's face it, doing it out loud is just plain awkward. But I learned quickly that there were two types of conversations I could have with myself: positive and uplifting conversations, or negative and destructive ones. I learned that the key to being successful came down to my own ability to limit those conversations in my head to the positive and uplifting ones.

Research has shown that it is our thoughts that drive our emotions, and our emotions that drive our actions. Therefore, if we want to act in a way that will bring us the most success, we have to control our emotions by learning to control our thoughts.

I find self-talk to be the most effective way to control my thoughts. When I find myself in a situation where I am feeling stressed or anxious or overwhelmed, I immediately begin having inner conversations with myself. If you were to jump inside my head, you would hear a typical conversation going something like this:

"I am seriously stressing out."

"Why are you stressing out?"

"Because I am never going to get everything done."

"All you can do is continue taking steps on what needs to get accomplished. There is absolutely nothing more you can possibly do, so take a deep breath and quit stressing, because stressing won't change anything here, it will only slow you down. Just keep moving forward doing the best you can do and it will all work out in the end."

"Good point, thanks."

It may sound silly to have that type of conversation with yourself, but I can tell you with certainty that it works. And the more you do it, the better you become at it. Think of it as having your own personal therapist with you twenty-four-seven, free of charge. Positive self-talk is one of the very best ways to improve your emotions and build your self-confidence.

Unfortunately, negative self-talk works just as effectively.

"I can't do it."

"I'm fat."

"I'm stupid."

When those are the types of things you're telling yourself repeatedly, you're bound to actually start believing them. You begin doubting yourself, and in turn you limit your actions, thus inhibiting your own success, which makes it imperative to learn to control your negative self-talk until you can stop it completely.

One way I have found to control my own negative self-talk is to immediately ask myself, "How would I feel if someone were saying that to my child?" That particular question is the perfect kick in the behind to help motivate me to snap out of it and change my thought pattern. If the voice in your head is saying something that you can't imagine saying to a person you love, then you shouldn't be saying it to yourself.

Another form of self-talk happens with our body language. This particular type of self-talk is one that we tend to overlook completely, yet it too has a powerful influence on our emotions. Have you ever observed yourself in the mirror while you're talking on the phone? If you haven't, I suggest you do. When we're watching ourselves in a mirror as we talk on the phone, we become far more engaged in our discussion, our voices sound different, and we reflect more concern. For this reason, I purchased small mirrors to put in the cubicles of each of my salespeople and customer service agents. As the employees observed themselves talking on the phone, they would communicate in a more caring and sincere way, and the results spoke for themselves.

Reading notes with self-talk can be even more powerful than reading motivational quotes and sayings from others. Try writing yourself a note on your bathroom mirror saying, for example, "You are going to ace your project today!" or "You can totally handle whatever challenges come your way." For some reason, when the advice is coming from you, to you, it seems to have an even greater influence on your thoughts and emotions.

Here is the self-talk litmus test: If you find yourself feeling unhappy or stressed out, you can bet that you've been subconsciously listening to your own negative self-talk.

Here is the self-talk litmus test: If you find yourself feeling unhappy or stressed out, you can bet that you've been subconsciously listening to your own negative self-talk. You've likely been telling yourself to expect the worst, that things are "always bad," or "never okay," or that everything is a horrible disaster—so of course you feel horrible! Who wouldn't feel horrible if someone followed them around all day criticizing everything they did? Yet we do it to ourselves, and we don't even notice we're doing it. If you feel like garbage, then your thoughts have been garbage, so take out the trash!

Tell the negative committee that meets inside your head to sit down and shut up!

—Ann Bradford

Change Your Perspective.

People often view the world around them in ways that are completely different from what's actually going on. I observed time and time again employees who interpreted something one way when the reality was actually totally different. I learned that when employees had only partial facts on a matter, they would read into the situation by taking those partial facts and mixing them with their own interpretation of other events—or their own emotions—and they blended these things together to come up with a world that they perceived to be true and factual.

I am not suggesting that this is something anyone does intentionally, but the reality is that I saw it happen almost every day as a CEO. Over time, it became clear to me that these misperceptions of the facts were causing unnecessary stress to employees and needless anxiety for their coworkers, so I decided to share some ideas with my employees on how they could avoid falling into the trap of interpreting situations with partial facts or partial understanding.

I started off by telling them a story that illustrates perfectly the way that all human beings tend to interpret the world around them, not just at work, but in everyday life.

A friend of mine had a son who committed suicide. She was absolutely devastated. She is one of the most amazing women I know and one of the best moms I've met. She is incredible, and no doubt her situation was both tragic and heartbreaking.

My friend shared that a few days after her son's suicide, she had to go to the store to pick something up. She was heartbroken and sad and could barely force herself to go out. As she arrived at the store, she saw everyone around her happy and hustling to get things done, and she said that with all her might she wanted to scream out "STOP! Don't you know what's happened? Don't you know that my son is dead? Don't you see that my world has come crashing down around me?"

Now imagine the perspective of another person who happened to be at the store that day, who had no idea what had just happened to my friend and who was in a hurry to just grab something and get out. This person got in line behind my friend—who was holding things up because she was preoccupied with thoughts of her loss and not paying attention—and they were so frustrated, thinking, "What is your problem? I'm in a hurry and you are holding me up! Why do you have to inconvenience everyone else because you can't get it together?!"

Rather than taking piecemeal information and painting the picture to be one that is negative or hurtful or sad, what if instead we took that same half information and chose to look for the positive meaning that might exist?

That story perfectly paints the picture of what happens every day around us. Someone views the events around them, and they immediately try to interpret those events using the data they have at that point, mixed with the emotions they are dealing with that day. They then form an opinion of a person or a situation and believe it to be true. And just like that, they have formed the way they see the world around them. How shocking would it be for everyone to suddenly have the entire story, all the facts, all the reasons, all the details—only to find out that everything they thought to be true wasn't the case at all?

The reality is that no one can ever have all the facts in every situation, because there just isn't time to gather them all. What we can do is modify the way that we choose to view things. Rather than taking piecemeal information and painting the picture to be one that is negative or hurtful or sad, what if instead we took that same half information and chose to look for the positive meaning that might exist? What if we chose to look for the way to view it in a light that was happy, and optimistic, and hopeful? Which of these two options is likely to help us feel the happiest?

Note the difference you can make by simply changing the way you perceive things:

- When someone is rude to those around them, instead of focusing on the fact that they are a jerk, consider that they might be feeling insecure and need validation to feel good about themselves, and offer a word of kindness.

- When someone is having a private conversation with someone else, instead of thinking they are talking negatively about you, consider being happy for them to be getting support from each other for whatever is going on in their lives.

- When a manager forgets to tell you they noticed your hard work, instead of thinking they don't appreciate all you do, consider that they might be overwhelmed themselves. Even though they didn't voice it, that doesn't mean they don't feel it, because their delegating or assigning to you is a clear sign that they need and trust you.

- When someone walks past you without saying hello, instead of thinking they don't like you, consider that they could just be running behind. Send good wishes their way to help them make it on time.

Don't allow yourself to interpret things negatively when the reality is that it's likely that 99.9 percent of the time they have nothing to do with you at all. If we all knew each other's backstory, we would clearly recognize the need we each have for one another's friendship, and we would give it far more generously.

Happiness comes with giving each other the benefit of the doubt. Choose to see the world through a positive interpretation. Choose to believe that people are good, with good hearts, and good intentions. Your perspective of the world is up to you. Make it beautiful.

Trials Should Make Us Better, Not Bitter.

Whether it's not getting a desired job, dealing with a difficult coworker, struggling to get along with a boss, hurting financially, coping with health problems, or nursing a damaged relationship, we all have to face adversity and trials in our lives. Sometimes the struggles we go through are the result of choices we made, and sometimes they are the result of events that were completely beyond our control. Regardless of the cause, no trial we experience or pain we suffer should be wasted. Trials educate us. They can build our character and help us develop patience, humility, and strength—if we choose to let them.

Years ago, I heard a speech given by a young, twenty-something woman who had grown up without sight or hearing. She underwent surgery in high school to have a cochlear implant, which partially restored her hearing and helped her to communicate her story more effectively. She was still totally blind. As she shared her life story with us, she asked us to close our eyes and imagine a world where all we saw was darkness, no color or light. She asked us to imagine how depressing that would feel. With eyes still closed, she then asked us to imagine our world with color and light and joy. She said, "The second picture you imagined is what I choose to see every day," and asked us to open our eyes. She proceeded to share with us that she had a choice in life, "to be sad and depressed and see only darkness, or to be happy and joyful and see color and light," and that she chose the latter, every day. She acknowledged that many times it is easy in life to focus on our trials.

"I often think that many of us count our blessings on our fingers and toes, but count our trials with a calculator," she said, describing how many of us spend our lives thinking, "Why me? Why is my life hard? Why am I having to struggle? Why do I have to suffer loss? Why, why, why?"

She proceeded to share with us that she had a choice in life, "to be sad and depressed and see only darkness, or to be happy and joyful and see color and light."

The words that came out of her mouth next caught me completely off guard.

"I too wake up each day and ask, 'Why me? Why am I so lucky to have ten fingers and ten toes? Why am I so lucky to have people who love me? Why am I so lucky to be able to walk? Why am I so blessed?'" My only thought was wow … just wow! She closed by reminding us that "all of us are given trials to make us better, not to make us bitter."

Her story was humbling beyond belief. I've been guilty at times of thinking "Why me?" in that "poor me" kind of way. And yet, here was this young woman coping with significantly harder challenges, and she was calling herself the lucky one.

In my life, I have been amazed at the strength of the people surrounding me. I have watched as people have overcome trials that I couldn't possibly imagine facing. I had one employee whose wife was on death's door for years. I had another employee whose young daughter struggled through years of chemotherapy battling cancer. I had another employee who suffered the loss of his eighteen-month-old baby. The list goes on and on. Each of them overcame their struggle with grace and humility, setting a powerful example for me, just as this young woman who'd spoken.

Each of us has it within us to overcome whatever trials are placed in our path. We can make the choice to see the light and joy in life rather than focusing on the dark. We can make the choice to learn from our trials, allowing them to refine our character and help us become a stronger, more charitable person. We can make the choice to be grateful, choosing to be joyful and seeing the color and light that blesses our life. We can make the choice to say, "Why me? Why am I so blessed?"

Though trials aren't fun and we want to avoid them, we have to remember that our greatest growth in life will never come from times of ease and comfort. Our greatest growth will come from those times we choose to overcome adversity and allow our trials to make us better.

CHAPTER 7

PEOPLE DO BUSINESS WITH PEOPLE THEY LIKE

The Two Most Powerful Words in Any Language

People will forget what you said. People will forget what you did. But people will never forget how you made them feel.

—*Maya Angelou*

People ultimately choose to do business with people they like, and everyone likes someone who appreciates them. Thus, the most powerful tool you have for creating success in your life is to appreciate other people.

When you appreciate others, you will find that your relationships are stronger, your circle of friends will grow wider, your career and business will succeed beyond your expectations, and your life will simply be happier. Who wouldn't want all of that? And how do we make that happen?

The two most powerful words in any language are "Thank you." Saying thank you communicates that you value and appreciate the other person. Saying thank you has the power to create friendships. Saying thank you has the influence to create loyalty. Saying thank you to everyone you come in contact with would make you one of the most beloved people in the world. But forgetting to say thank you leaves the other person feeling taken for granted and unappreciated, and one can easily surmise the damage those feelings would do toward building future bonds.

Now that we all agree on the importance of saying thank you, let's talk about a few tips on how to say it best.

When saying thank you, it is best to be specific about what exactly you are thankful for. When you take time to do so, you are helping that employee feel appreciated, but at the same time you are also teaching them the behaviors they should repeat in order to receive further thanks in the future. For example, a manager might say to an employee who did a good job on an assignment, "Thank you for the attention you paid to the smallest details on this project! I realize you put in extra

When saying thank you, it is best to be specific about what exactly you are thankful for.

hours to get this completed so smoothly and I truly appreciate your efforts." That employee will walk away feeling appreciated as well as knowing that paying attention to detail and going the extra mile are behavior patterns they want to continue to follow in order to receive future praise.

Saying thank you to someone out of the blue, in an unexpected moment, can also make a huge impact on them. For example, when someone has done nothing in the present moment that calls for thanks, just stop and say thank you to them for something they exemplify, such as, "Thank you for always setting an example of integrity with your life." Those unexpected thank-yous can make a lasting impression.

One of the most powerful forms of appreciation is when you take the time to say thank you to someone in a handwritten note. As a CEO, I found time and again that the most valued gift I could give someone was a handwritten note of thanks, and the only items I have saved without fail over the years are the handwritten notes of thanks that employees and clients sent to me. There is something so deeply personal and meaningful in a handwritten note of appreciation. At my past company, we had thousands of thank-you cards with the company logo printed for the employees to write and mail handwritten thank-you notes to our clients, our vendors, and each other. The value created over the years from these simple handwritten notes didn't equal millions of dollars, but rather hundreds of millions of dollars, because the notes helped us to grow our company to levels beyond expectations because of the close personal bonds with our clients and service providers they helped to foster.

We all have hundreds of opportunities to say thank you each day. We can thank the woman behind the counter at the gas station who rings us up when we grab our morning diet soda. We can thank the person in the drive-through who hands us our lunch order. We can thank the person who holds the door open for us when we walk into the building. If you pay attention for one day to everyone who could possibly deserve to hear "thank you," you will be amazed at the number of opportunities that can be missed if you aren't watching for them.

There is never a downside to saying thank you to someone. It can only make your own life and the lives of those around you better. So with that, let me say "thank you" for being who you are.

Now get out there and BE LIKEABLE!

The Fastest Way to Achieve Success Is to First Help Others Succeed.

Successful people are always looking for opportunities to help others. Unsuccessful people are always asking, "What's in it for me?"

—Brian Tracy

Without a doubt, the fastest way to achieve success is to first help others succeed. Yet there seems to be a belief in the business world that the only way to get ahead is to only watch out for "number one." That is simply not the case. The fact is that our greatest successes in life often come through helping others to succeed, and without question, when you focus on helping others succeed, your eventual payoff will always be far greater than your investment.

Here are five ways that everyone can help others to succeed, and in turn find greater success themselves:

1. **Pay attention to the details of other people's lives:** When you make the effort to remember the important details of others' lives, such as their spouse's name, their children, their hobbies, and so on, your ability to be a positive impact in their life increases tremendously. It lets the other person know how important they are to you. It lets them know that you truly care about their life. The more a person knows that you genuinely care about them, the more they will, in turn, move heaven and earth to help you with the things you want. And with the contact tracking tools available on our electronic devices today, it is incredibly simple to make quick notes about people so that your memory is always fresh.

   Our greatest successes in life often come through helping others to succeed.

2. **Help people connect by sharing your network with others:** Be willing to introduce people to others you know who can help advance or forward their goals. When you have a networking event to attend, invite people to come with you who could benefit from expanding their network as well. The more you open up your network to others, the more you will find your own network expanding, and you might be amazed at the incredible contacts you end up receiving from the most unlikely people.

3. **Inspiring a person is worth far more than motivating a person:** You can motivate an employee with a raise or a fancy title, and for a time they will feel motivated to work harder to

show their appreciation. But after a while, they begin to forget the additional money and the fancier title, because those have now become the "norm," and you'll find that once again they are back to needing added motivation to take their performance to the next level. On the other hand, if you inspire an employee by treating them with respect and frequently letting them know, in a sincere way, just how much you appreciate them and the contribution they are making, you will find that they are constantly motivated to increase their efforts. Inspiring others is the ultimate form of perpetual motivation.

4. **Give honest feedback in a respectful and constructive way:** This is one of the most difficult things for people to learn to do well. Many people don't like confronting issues and would rather dance around them, while those who do like confrontation often aren't respectful or constructive in the way they give feedback. But those who do learn the skill of giving honest and open feedback in a constructive and uplifting way can have a tremendous positive impact on the lives of others. One mental trick that has helped me with giving feedback is always making sure I am walking into the conversation with the mind-set of truly caring about the person and genuinely wanting to help them improve. If I go into the conversation with that motivation, then my words naturally come out better. The more you give feedback to help others improve, the more you will find that they in turn will open up to you and give you feedback that helps you improve as well.

5. **Be willing to put the needs of others first, even when it means you have to overlook your own wants:** Simon Sinek once said, "Marine leaders are expected to eat last because the

true price of leadership is the willingness to place the needs of others above your own." This particular point can be one of the most difficult things to actually do in the moment, because it feels so counterintuitive to put others' needs above your own when doing so appears to require you to set aside your own desires. But as counterintuitive as it sounds, the fact is that it genuinely works—perhaps not instantly, but over time it leads to getting

Those who do learn the skill of giving honest and open feedback in a constructive and uplifting way can have a tremendous positive impact on the lives of others.

you everything you want and more. I can say this with absolute conviction, because I have seen it in my own life. The more I focused on helping my employees to personally succeed both in their professional and personal lives, the more my entire company succeeded—and as a result, I personally succeeded far more than I ever would have imagined.

The more we serve our fellowmen in appropriate ways, the more substance there is to our souls. We become more significant individuals … Indeed, it is easier to "find" ourselves because there is so much more of us to find!

—*Spencer W. Kimball*

Showing Compassion Creates a Ripple Effect.

Compassion is not religious business, it is human business.

—The Dalai Lama

Compassion. It is a word we often hear talked about when it comes to religion, but it is not a word used often enough when it comes to discussing what makes a business successful. Yet compassion can directly affect the bottom line. Compassion helps leaders be successful, it helps employees become successful, and ultimately it contributes to making companies a success.

Multiple studies have shown that acts of compassion, kindness, and generosity create a ripple effect that stems from those who do the act and moves to those who observe it, and that ripple continues expanding, impacting numerous others who all benefit as a result of just one single act of compassion. At the conclusion of one particular study, James Fowler of UC San Diego and Nicolas Christakis of Harvard reported, "The results suggest that each additional contribution a subject makes to the public good in the first period is tripled over the course of the experiment by other subjects who are directly or indirectly influenced to contribute more as a consequence. These results show experimentally that cooperative behavior cascades in human social networks." They go on to say that "as a result, each person in a network can influence dozens or even hundreds of people, some of whom he or she does not know and has not met."[5]

If a single show of compassion can have that far reaching of an impact, just imagine the enormous impact an entire company of people showing compassion can have. All it takes is one person willing to take the lead.

When a leader creates a "ripple," it has the power to affect the greatest number of people in their organization. Research performed at Stanford University has revealed that our relationship with a direct manager is probably the primary influence on the quality of our workplace experience, yet many managers still overlook the centrality of compassion to their role.

In a recent article, Emma Seppala, associate director of the Center for Compassion and Altruism Research and Education at Stanford University, said, "Managers may shy away from compassion for fear of appearing weak. Yet history is filled with leaders who were highly compassionate and very powerful—Mother Teresa, Martin Luther King, and Desmond Tutu, to name a few. They were such strong and inspiring leaders that people would drop everything to follow

> **If a single show of compassion can have that far reaching of an impact, just imagine the enormous impact an entire company of people showing compassion can have. All it takes is one person willing to take the lead.**

---

5   James H. Fowler and Nicholas A. Christakis, "Cooperative behavior cascades in human social networks," *PNAS* 107, no. 12 (March 23, 2010): 5334-5338, https://doi.org/10.1073/pnas.0913149107.

them. Wouldn't any manager wish for that kind of loyalty and commitment?"[6]

Simply put, a leader who desires to succeed cannot afford to overlook the importance of showing compassion, nor can they discount the impact their example will be on the entire organization of people they lead.

Showing compassion doesn't have to be a burden. It simply entails showing sympathy and mercy for another—trying to understand other people's needs and helping them in the ways you are able. Let me share a personal experience that taught me how simple it can be for a leader to influence the level of compassion in a company:

I noticed over the holidays that we always had some employees who seemed to be doing quite well in life and others who were going through tougher times. As I pondered ways I could be of help, I realized that as the leader I had the ability to get the employees focused on helping each other over the holidays by launching what we called our "Santa Store." We decided that each year during the holiday season we would ask employees to go through their belongings at home and contribute any items they no longer needed to the company Santa Store. Then every employee could take any items from the store that they needed. Thus employees got the chance to both give and receive.

We had employees donating everything from kids clothing to adult clothing, to toys, DVDs, video games, winter coats, gloves, computers, bicycles, televisions, DVD players, furniture, books, games ... you name it, we had it donated. All of these items were set up on tables in a room, and then the room was left open for employees

6 Emma Seppala, "Compassion In Business Benefits Employers And Employees, Workplace Stress Research Shows," Huffington Post, last modified December 6, 2017, https://www.huffingtonpost.com/2013/08/06/compassion-in-business-makes-sense_n_3684661.html.

to go through and take anything they needed for their families. We set no limit on what an employee could take from the store. We only asked that they limit what they took to the things they needed for themselves or their own families so that we could make sure our employees' families were taken care of first. Then once employees had time to take everything they needed for themselves, we made all the leftover items available for employees to take and give to anyone else they knew who was in need that year. The Santa Store became a huge benefit to the employees, but it didn't stop there.

As employees were involved in this showing and receiving of compassion from one another, the entire morale of the company began to improve. People were happier at work, they were kinder to one another, and then suddenly that ripple effect began spreading beyond the walls of our company. As employees were on the phones talking to customers, they were showing an increased level of care and concern for the clients. Their efforts to understand the needs of the customer became more personal to them, and they became more dedicated to doing whatever they could to help that customer feel happy. Employees began sending personal handwritten notes of thanks to clients, and seemed happy to go the extra mile to take care of them.

As you can imagine, the clients were thrilled by this level of compassion being extended to them, and over time we saw these clients begin to go the extra mile for us as well. They began referring more business to us, both from their own organization as well as from other organizations. As a result, our company began to grow and flourish in ways we couldn't have imagined, and the impact to our bottom line was amazing.

Change your focus, from making money to serving more people. Serving more people makes the money come in.

—Robert Kiyosaki

Indeed, serving each other inside the organization with an increased showing of compassion led to serving clients outside the organization with increased showings of compassion and that ripple effect bounced off of them and came rippling right back to us tenfold.

Serving each other inside the organization with increased compassion led to serving clients with increased compassion, which then bounced off of them and came rippling right back to us tenfold.

We've all heard Winston Churchill's quote, "We make a living by what we get, but we make a life by what we give."

But I would also submit to you that what we give by showing compassion not only makes our lives better, it can make our livings better as well.

Be Openly Vulnerable. It Can Be Your Most Valuable Asset.

I've learned many lessons through my years of leading companies, but without question, the most surprising thing I learned was this: the thing that will make you the strongest is the thing that seems the most counterintuitive to do—be openly vulnerable.

I am sure many of you are scratching your head, thinking I have lost my mind, especially because we have all been trained to think that being vulnerable means being weak, which is the exact opposite of strong. So why then, would I suggest that being openly vulnerable is the very thing that will actually make you strong?

Trust me, I get why you would think it's crazy, because many years ago I would have thought the same thing. Being vulnerable was not my strong suit growing up. In my mind, being vulnerable meant being weak and available to be hurt, so I learned to hide my fears and to always act with confidence, which in many ways served me well, because it helped me to put myself out there and try new things that I might not otherwise have been willing to try. It was that "I can do anything" attitude that likely led me to become an entrepreneur back when it appeared that all the odds were stacked against me. Being openly vulnerable wasn't even a consideration back then, and I would even say that I went to great lengths to avoid it.

But, as is often the case, life began teaching me some very valuable lessons as I was running my first business. Not allowing myself to appear vulnerable meant I had to be perfect at everything. I had to be in control of everything, because that was the only way to have the outcome turn out according to my perfect plans. It was exhausting. Not only was it exhausting for me, but it created a miserable situation for the people I was leading. You see, if leaders can't allow themselves to be vulnerable then they send a clear message that no one who works for them is allowed to be vulnerable either. Leaders who expect perfection from themselves are sending the message that they expect only perfection from those around them as well. It is an impossible expectation for anyone to live up to—both for the leader as well as the people they are responsible to lead—

because the reality is that no one is perfect. No one. And try as we may in this life, none of us will ever get there, because we are only human, and as such we are by nature imperfect beings all striving to improve ourselves to the best of our ability.

I finally began to recognize that my unwillingness to show vulnerability as a leader was causing everyone around me to feel inadequate, and that was the last thing I wanted. My passion in life and my personal mission statement is "to help others to excel," yet here I was creating an atmosphere that didn't allow anyone to excel, including me, because my lack of vulnerability meant that anything less than perfection was failure. I was instantly making all of us failures. I finally figured out that something had to change, and that something was me—it was time for me embrace being vulnerable.

If leaders can't allow themselves to be vulnerable, they send a clear message that no one who works for them is allowed to be vulnerable either.

I can't say that "being vulnerable" takes courage, because every one of us is vulnerable whether we acknowledge it or not. We are all vulnerable to disappointment, sadness, sickness, death, loss, failure, losing our job, losing love, and so on. But embracing our vulnerability, and even more important, openly embracing it ... well, that does take courage, and lots of it. But it was through embracing my own vulnerability and admitting to my employees and clients that I was imperfect—and making mistakes that I was learning and growing from—that I was able to become a strong leader. What made me strong was the support of those very people, who, knowing I needed them, were willing to support me and stand by me and help me in my efforts to become a better leader and to lead our company to success.

People who won't embrace vulnerability are simply not being authentic. They project a message of "I am perfect and you are not, so how then can we ever relate?" But if a person is admittedly imperfect and so are you, then you instantly have a bond that allows you to relate to one another, and a connection is formed. It is those connections that will cause people to give you their very best efforts, because they want to help you succeed. It is also those connections that will cause people to look to you as someone they can learn from because you have now given them permission to try and fail and grow from it, just as you have. You are setting an attainable example for others to follow, and it is one that will truly allow them to excel.

It takes courage to admit that you are not perfect. It takes courage to acknowledge that you cannot control the outcomes, especially when your entire job is to produce outcomes. But all of those things are true whether you admit to them or not, so why not embrace them? We will never achieve perfection, so the most we can do is live our lives in the honest pursuit of it. We can never control the outcomes, so the most we can do is live our lives controlling our best efforts. We will never control how others feel about us or treat us, so the most we can do is control our ability to love others and treat them well.

PART III

LEADING THE RIGHT WAY

CHAPTER 8

THE INSPIRED LEADER

The Characteristics of a True Leader

True leaders understand that leadership is not about them but about those they serve. It is not about exalting themselves but about lifting others up.

—*Sheri L. Dew*

123

Every one of us is a leader in our own right. Whether we lead an entire company, or a team of people, or a group of friends, or our families, or just ourselves, we are all leaders in some form or fashion. Whatever size our circle of influence may be today, if we work to improve as leaders, that circle of influence will enlarge.

I have been in positions of leadership my entire career, and during those years I have learned much about the difference between being a bad leader and being a good leader. Some lessons I learned the hard way, through trial and error followed by the humility that comes from overcoming those mistakes. Other lessons I learned through observing those I esteemed to be great leaders whose example I sought to follow. Through it all, I found several traits that I believe are necessary for someone to be what I consider a true leader:

- **True leaders know who they are and what they stand for.** They know their values and the rules they will abide by, regardless of the circumstances they face. They help their people understand the values they are committed to uphold, and that lays a foundation for the rules their people will be expected to adhere to. True leaders both know and communicate their values openly with the people they lead, creating an atmosphere of certainty and trust.

- **True leaders have integrity.** Integrity is the very core of their influence. Living the values they profess to believe is what gives them credibility and allows others to place their trust in them. True leaders are able to say "Do as I do" rather than just "Do as I say," because they lead by example.

- **True leaders work right alongside the people they lead in order to get to know and care about the people they are**

leading. Working with people allows leaders to lift and inspire their team.

- **True leaders listen without being condescending.** They are willing to hear what others have to say without rushing to judgment. They are patient and genuine in their desire to understand the thoughts and feelings of the people they lead.

> **True leaders work right alongside the people they lead in order to get to know and care about the people they are leading.**

- **True leaders are forthright with their people.** They communicate openly and often. True leaders take the time to communicate often to their team to show that their team is valued and important to them. They understand that as the leader they have an obligation to communicate directly with their people so that they never allow a void that someone with mal-intent can fill. True leaders take on the responsibility of communicating for themselves.

- **True leaders reprimand their people from a place of love and a genuine desire to help them improve.** They reprimand without anger, and they relay feedback in a direct yet kind and respectful way. Even when they see a bad behavior needing to be corrected, they don't view the person doing the behavior as a bad person. They listen and attempt to understand what led to that person making the mistake or exhibiting the bad behavior in order to understand the underlying cause that needs correcting. True leaders understand that when a person feels valued and cared for by their leader, they are far more willing to take the feedback and implement the needed changes. They understand that using those communication styles break people's trust and leave them feeling uncertain or belittled, and ultimately lead to harboring bad feelings toward their leader—none of which inspire a desire to change or improve their own behavior.

- **True leaders don't control their people, they inspire them to do great things.** They give them the values and rules, which set the boundaries to operate within. Then they encourage people to go out and make choices on their own. True leaders understand that employees cannot grow and progress until they are given the freedom to make choices, try things, and yes, even make a few mistakes so that they can learn from them and improve.

- **True leaders delegate.** They give important and specific tasks to their people to help them learn and grow in their positions. Often it would be far easier for the leader to simply do the task themselves—they could get it done more quickly, more effectively, and exactly to their liking. However, true leaders understand that doing so allows no growth for the people they are leading, and therefore they see their greatest role as a delegator and a teacher to the people they lead.

- **True leaders are not afraid to make demands of the people they lead.** True leaders understand that it is a mistake to be too soft, just as it is a mistake to be too harsh. They have the courage to direct their team in the work that needs to get accomplished, expressing their belief in their people's abilities, delegating duties, and teaching and correcting their people along the way. They help employees grow by making reasonable but real demands. They don't assign people tasks that are beyond their ability, but they do assign tasks that cause them to stretch themselves. They recognize the possibilities of what their team can accomplish, and they motivate each person to recognize their potential.

- **True leaders use their time wisely.** That doesn't mean they can't take time for leisure and fun; it simply means they do their best not to waste the time they have. They are selfless, and they work tirelessly to help make their team a success.

- **True leaders hold themselves and their people accountable.** They hold themselves to a high standard, so they can hold their people to a high standard as well.

- **True leaders keep things in perspective.** They don't rush into making short-term decisions that will benefit their organization today only to cause even greater problems in the future. They try to take all the facts into account, keeping a long-term view, with the desire that any fixes they put in place today will be to the benefit of the organization and the people, both now and in the future.

We all have room to improve as leaders, but our ultimate goal should be the same: to be leaders who are loved, admired, and respected by the people we lead as we motivate and inspire them to achieve their full potential.

Good Employees Make Mistakes, Great Leaders Allow Them To.

As a business leader, I found that one of the scariest things was to give my people the freedom to make mistakes. While mistakes allow individuals to learn and grow, they can also be very costly. Scared as I was, I knew that truly great leaders found ways to allow their people to take these risks, and I genuinely wanted to be a great leader. I wanted to help my employees grow, so I set out to discover how to accomplish this without placing my company in jeopardy.

> *Courage is not the absence of fear, but rather the judgment that something else is more important than fear.*
>
> —Ambrose Redmoon

I quickly discovered there were two steps I needed to take. The first was to determine the areas of the business where a mistake would not cause too much damage. I took careful attention to make sure any areas where we would damage our clients and the trust they had placed in us were off limits for significant risk without serious executive involvement and oversight. I identified other areas where I could feel more comfortable allowing people the freedom to experiment on new and better ways of doing things.

The second step was to communicate to the employees that we were setting an official company policy: Making any mistake once was okay, so long as it was an honest mistake made while attempting to do what they felt was the right thing. But repeating that same mistake a second time was *not* okay. The hard, fast rule was that if you made any mistake the first time, the entire team would have your back in fixing it if anything went wrong. However, if you ever repeated that mistake, you would face the consequences 100 percent on your own.

We all make mistakes—every one of us. If we aren't making mistakes, we likely aren't trying enough new things outside our comfort zone—and that itself is a mistake, robbing you of the best way to learn and grow as a person. As John Wooden once said, "If you're not making mistakes, then you're not doing anything." Mistakes are the pathway to great ideas and innovation. Mistakes are the stepping stones leading out of the comfort zone and into the growing zone, where new discoveries are made and great lessons are learned. Mistakes are not failures; they are simply the process of eliminating ways that won't work in order to come closer to the ways that will.

> **Mistakes are the stepping stones leading out of the comfort zone and into the growing zone, where new discoveries are made and great lessons are learned.**

Great leaders allow their people the freedom to make mistakes. But good employees are those who, when mistakes are made, (1) learn from them, (2) own them, (3) fix them, and (4) put safeguards in place to ensure the same mistake will never be repeated again.

The Steps to Correcting Mistakes

1. **Learn from them:** Good employees recognize when they have made an honest mistake. They do not get defensive about it, but instead are willing to look objectively at their mistake,

recognize what they did wrong, and understand why their choice or actions were the wrong thing to do.

2. **Own them:** Good employees take accountability for their mistakes. They admit them readily. They don't make excuses for a mistake, but instead acknowledge that yes, they made a mistake, and they express openly what lesson they have learned from that mistake.

3. **Fix them:** Good employees do what it takes to rectify their wrongs. They do all they can to fix it and make it right. Certainly there are times when the damage is done and recompense cannot be made, but good employees do their very best to repair whatever damage has been done to the best of their ability. They always establish a timeline with follow up for when the problem will be fixed, and make sure that progress is communicated so that everyone feels the urgency and care with which they are correcting the problem.

4. **Put safeguards in place to ensure the same mistake will never be repeated:** This is the most critical step in the learning process. When a mistake has clearly been made, the most important thing anyone can do is figure out what safety nets and roadblocks can be established to ensure that this same mistake will not happen again. Document this step so that the lessons learned and the safeguards set up can always go beyond you. Do everything in your power to help others learn from your mistake so that they don't have to experience it firsthand.

The steps in correcting mistakes apply to any area of life. Whether it's business life, home life, or personal life, the principles of apologizing remain the same. Good employees make a lot of mistakes, and truly great employees are those who have mastered the art of apologizing for those mistakes.

The Six A's of a Proper Apology

1. **Admit**—I made a mistake.

2. **Apologize**—I am sorry for making the mistake.

3. **Acknowledge**—I recognize where I went wrong that caused my mistake to occur.

4. **Attest**—I plan to do the following to fix the mistake, on this specific timeline.

5. **Assure**—I will put the following protections in place to ensure that I do not make the same mistake again.

6. **Abstain**—Never repeat the same mistake twice.

People who implement the six A's will find that the level of trust and respect others have for them will grow tenfold. People who implement the six A's will find that others will be quicker to forgive them and more likely to extend a second chance. It's not the making of a mistake that is generally the problem; it's what you do with it afterward that really counts.

Admitting You Were Wrong Doesn't Make You Weak— It Makes You Awesome.

It takes tremendous fortitude to utter the words "I was wrong, and I am sorry." I love that word: fortitude. I could list the dictionary definition, but why go to that trouble when there's Microsoft Word's handy one-click synonym function, which in fortitude's case gives us: strength, courage, resilience, grit, determination, endurance, guts, and staying power. Booyah! Who doesn't want to be all of that?!

So often in business, I deal with people who believe that admitting they were wrong shows weakness or ineptness. The danger of that belief, especially when it is held by people in positions of power or authority, is that it backs a leader into defending their poor choices even when they themselves have come to recognize they were wrong. These managers end up placing false blame on others to prove that they were right. They point fingers and say that someone else didn't execute as they should have and that is the reason things went wrong. In their minds, they see this as a way to save face, or to prove they are deserving of their power, or to retain respect for their intelligence. Sadly, they don't accomplish any of those things. In fact, they accomplish the exact opposite.

The best employees in the organization recognize when mistakes have been made, and they also recognize when a manager is covering their own tracks. They ultimately lose respect, trust, and confidence in the manager, and more often than not they will jump ship at the first opportunity to work in a better environment.

I don't know exactly why so many in the world carry the false belief that admitting their mistakes makes them weak, but I can tell you how I learned to recognize that the opposite is true.

I was somewhere in my twenties visiting the home of a family in California when I witnessed a heated disagreement between the father of the home and his defiant preteen daughter. There was no question that the lesson the father was trying to teach the daughter was a correct one, but the way he handled it was not. He didn't strike his daughter or become abusive, but his tone was hurtful and degrading.

After the incident ended, knowing the man well, I thought to myself, *He has to know that wasn't right, because I know him to be a good man. But there is no way he would admit it, because he doesn't want to lose face as the leader of the family.* I wouldn't say that one incident made me lose all respect for the man, because I knew his character better than that, and I knew of his incredible qualities, but I clearly recognized that he was in the wrong. About an hour later, I walked down the hall to hear the man saying these exact words to his daughter: "I was wrong, and I am sorry."

I was honestly shocked. I had never before heard someone in authority admit they were wrong and apologize like that. He made no excuse for his behavior. He gave no justification, such as "Well, I only acted like that because you did this." Nothing, nada, zip. He simply admitted he was wrong and apologized. Observing his behavior, my respect for this man grew tremendously. I saw him as a great leader and a person of fortitude that I wanted to be like.

Seeing his behavior that day changed my life, because I recognized that the reason I now saw him as a leader of great fortitude was his willingness to honestly and humbly admit his mistake, especially to someone subordinate to him.

If we want to be genuinely successful in both business and life, we have to be willing to set aside our pride, our fears, and our insecurities, and really come to recognize that to be a true leader who is deserving of our position of authority, we must earn—not demand—the respect of our coworkers. The journey toward earning their respect begins the moment we recognize our mistakes and have the integrity and fortitude to utter the words "I was wrong, and I am sorry."

> **The journey toward earning their respect begins the moment we recognize our mistakes and have the integrity and fortitude to utter the words "I was wrong, and I am sorry."**

You Can Put Your Mistakes Behind You.

People often think they can't change their past, but I disagree. Perhaps we can't change every mistake in our past, but we have to remember that the past is a moving target. Every day that goes by becomes a part of our past history. Whatever we do today will become a part of our past tomorrow, which means that we do have the power to change our past—by doing the right things today. Today we have the ability to continue building on our past story, and that gives us the power to modify that story into one we can be proud of. It's important to remember that the whole of our past is far more powerful than any of its parts.

I've already talked about the importance of leaders allowing their employees the room to make mistakes in order to help them grow and improve, and I shared the six A's of a proper apology when we do make a mistake. As a follow-up to that, I think it is important to discuss what happens after we've made a mistake and a proper apology has been given. How do we move forward and put that mistake in our past? How do we keep that mistake from freezing us with fears of repeat failure? How do we keep that mistake from eroding our confidence?

Those are incredibly important questions, because without the answers, we can easily get sucked into a never-ending state of dwelling on our past mistakes, reliving them in our head, and feeling like a constant failure. Our self-esteem and confidence can be sucked away, and it can make us hesitant to try again for fear of falling flat on our face and revisiting that feeling of failure. Having the answers on how to move past our mistakes in a positive, healthy way is critical to our future success.

The first thing that will help put a mistake in the past is to ensure that all six A's of a proper apology were completed with whomever the mistake impacted or damaged: admit, apologize, acknowledge, attest, assure, and abstain. There is a feeling of confidence that comes from having the courage to take ownership of our mistakes this way. It also shows others that we have fortitude and a desire to make things right, and it opens a door to allow us to regain any trust that may have been lost, helping to restore our own confidence in the process.

The second thing that will help is to let it go. If we have done the six A's of a proper apology and we are committed to not repeating the mistake, it is time to let it go. There is nothing more frustrating and discouraging than being around someone who constantly points out our past mistakes to us. It makes us angry and hurt, and frankly it makes us want to avoid the people who do that to us. So why are we so willing to be the very person who is the most up in our own face about our mistakes, who points them out the very loudest, who beats us up the very most for how stupid our past mistakes were? Especially when it is impossible to avoid our own self! No wonder our self-esteem and our confidence take such a beating when we make a mistake. We cannot move forward if we allow ourselves to stay stuck in quicksand—it ain't gonna happen. We can't keep bringing our mistakes up to others, and we sure as heck can't keep bringing them up to ourselves by thinking about them, dwelling on them, and allowing our thoughts to beat us down. Instead, we need to say to ourselves, "Yeah, everyone gets it. I made a mistake, but I did what I could to fix it. Now it is time to let go and move on!"

That lesson is taught best in the Disney movie *The Lion King*. There is a point in the movie when the young lion Simba is feeling

Decide now what ideals you are going to stand for in your life, and then go into each day determined to stand by them no matter what comes your way.

sorry for himself for his past mistakes. The wise baboon Rafiki takes a stick and hits Simba on the back of the head. Simba yells, "Geez, what was that for?" and Rafiki replies, "It doesn't matter, it's in the past." Simba says, "Yeah, but it still hurts." Rafiki then says, "Oh yes, the past can hurt. But the way I see it, you can either run from it, or ... learn from it." Rafiki swings the stick again to hit Simba on the head, but now Simba ducks down in time to avoid the stick. Rafiki says, "You see." I love this example! It's the perfect reminder that this principle should not be a difficult one for us to grasp. Yes, it hurts to mess up, but it's in the past, so learn from it and move on.

There is no question that making mistakes is a necessary part of our growing process, but I do believe there is a way that we can still learn and grow without making quite so many mistakes, and in a way that can be far less painful. Decide now what ideals you are going to stand for in your life, and then go into each day determined to stand by them no matter what comes your way. It is amazing how much uncertainty disappears from our life when we know in advance what we want to stand for. Decisions become easier, temptations weaken, and our confidence grows, all of which allow us to put our mistakes in the past and move forward far more quickly, confidently, and successfully. And when you do make your next mistake—which, like all of us, you most certainly will—own it, fix it, and for heaven's sake, when that stick comes swinging toward the back of your head, hopefully you have learned enough to duck!

CHAPTER 9

A LEADER PEOPLE WANT TO FOLLOW

Good Leaders Are Invaluable to a Company. Bad Leaders Will Destroy It.

Become the kind of leader that people would follow voluntarily; even if you had no title or position.

—Brian Tracy

When good leadership is in place in a company, it can be felt throughout the entire organization. With good leadership, corporate culture isn't forced, it is developed. Communication is daily and open. Everyone understands the vision and goals of the organization, and everyone has input into how they can be improved. Employees feel that they are an important part of the whole and that every job matters. Decisions for promotions are based on picking people of integrity whose talents and experience best fit the positions. Employees are encouraged to compete with their own best to get ahead and they understand that helping their coworkers to succeed is the best way to get ahead themselves. The result of good leadership is high morale, good employee retention, and sustainable long-term success.

> *A true leader has the confidence to stand alone, the courage to make tough decisions, and the compassion to listen to the needs of others. He does not set out to be a leader, but becomes one by the equality of his actions and the integrity of his intent.*
>
> —*Douglas MacArthur*

Bad leadership can also be felt throughout the entire organization—only not in a good way. Under bad leadership, corporate culture becomes a meaningless term where leaders claim it exists while employees shake their heads in frustration. There is a lack of clear, consistent communication from leadership to the employees. As a result, the office is run by rumor mill, politics, and gamesmanship. Employees are uncertain of the company's goals and objectives for success and they have no idea how they fit into that picture, or what their level of importance is in making it happen. Decisions for promotions are not based on integrity or talent, but rather on who can talk the biggest talk or who is deemed the least threatening to the current leadership team. Employees are taught to play dirty against coworkers to get ahead by watching as leadership rewards that behavior in others, leading to the lobster syndrome of tearing one another

Under bad leadership, corporate culture becomes a meaningless term where leaders claim it exists while employees shake their heads in frustration.

down throughout the organization. The result of bad leadership is low morale, high turnover, and a decreased ability to have any sustainable success.

> *You don't lead by hitting people over the head—that's assault, not leadership.*
>
> *—Dwight Eisenhower*

To become a truly great company it takes truly great leaders. And there is a huge difference in bosses and leaders.

Companies cannot afford to have poor leadership if they want to truly succeed—and I don't just mean in terms of financial success. I define success as far more than just money. I define success for a company as having a good product or service that adds value to the lives of its customers, while providing a positive working environment that allows employees to grow and flourish in their talents and abilities as well as their personal value system, all while generating a profitable return for shareholders. If a company isn't doing all of those, then it isn't truly successful.

DIFFERENCE BETWEEN	
BOSS	**LEADER**
Drives employees	Coaches employees
Depends on authority	Depends on goodwill
Inspires fear	Generates enthusiasm
Says, "I"	Says, "We"
Places blame for the breakdown	Fixes the breakdown
Knows how it is done	Shows how it is done
Uses people	Develops people
Takes credit	Gives credit
Commands	Asks
Says, "Go"	Says, "Let's go"

Employees cannot flourish under poor leadership, and when employees do have to follow poor leaders, companies risk losing their very best and most talented people. Don't risk allowing poor leaders to lead your organization. For anyone who is ever granted the opportunity to take a leadership position, remember that being a true leader doesn't come from a title; it is a designation you must earn from the people you lead.

Feedback: Give It, Invite It, and Receive It

When someone isn't performing well at their job, or when they aren't the right fit for a particular position, or when their personality isn't a match for the company culture, one of the biggest disservices you can do to them is to not tell them the truth.

I found that one of the toughest things to teach people that serve in a management role is how to give honest feedback to others. I found that they were often afraid to hurt feelings, or they were afraid of not being liked. Rather than giving direct, honest feedback, they would sugarcoat things and dance around an issue. One of my least favorite things they would do is try to pass the problem off to another manager in another department as a way to avoid having to take care of the situation themselves.

For many years, I struggled with how to help people become comfortable in giving honest feedback. It was difficult, because I had also struggled to give direct feedback in my earlier years as a leader, so I understood what they were going through and why it was hard for them. But I also knew how important it was for me to teach them to do it, because I had learned firsthand the positive impact that came from learning to tell people the truth directly. I had seen the difference between situations where I avoided telling someone straight up what needed to change, and situations where I had been willing to overcome my fears and just put truth out there for the other person to hear.

Throughout this process, I learned seven very important lessons:

1. As a leader, you have an obligation to set the example of giving honest and direct feedback to employees. If you don't do it, no one else will either, so it must start with you.

2. Never feel guilty telling someone else the truth about what isn't working or what has to change. They deserve to know it. They cannot change and improve unless they know the truth about what they are doing wrong. You owe it to them to be honest and open.

3. Always give feedback from a position of truly wanting to help the other person with the information. Never give feedback at a time you are angry or frustrated, or you will end up tearing the other person down and no good will come from it. If you enter into the conversation with the genuine desire to help the other person to improve and grow, your heart will be in the right place, and your words will come out in a way that builds, not destroys.

4. It is okay to start the conversation by telling the other person that what you need to discuss with them is a little uncomfortable for you, but you also know that it's in their best interest for you to give them honest feedback, so you are going to do your best to do so. This lets the other person know that your intentions are good, and it helps stop them from becoming immediately defensive and allows them to be more open to what you have to tell them.

5. Be very clear in explaining exactly what they need to do differently. Don't just talk in broad, general terms. Give them specific examples of what they have done wrong and then give them an example of how they could have handled things differently. Keep in mind that most people are not trying to

mess up or be difficult. They are usually either unaware of their own bad behavior, or they are frustrated because they can't figure out how to do it differently. Typically, they will appreciate having some practical examples that teach them new ways to approach things.

6. Always be honest with respect. If you talk to the other person in a way that demonstrates your respect for them, they will appreciate your words far more, and you will have a far better chance of making an impact with them.

7. Make sure that anytime you share something negative, you also take time to express the positive. Let the person know what they are doing right as well as what they are doing wrong. You want people to walk away knowing that not everything they do is bad, and you want them to recognize the good things they should continue to do.

As a manager, you are speaking to a person who is just as nervous about having the conversation as you are. Recognize that you are in a position to affect their livelihood. That can be nerve-racking for the other person, so go out of your way to make it as comfortable a conversation as possible. As you are giving them feedback, be sure to ask if there are things you could be doing better as their leader to help them as they are

An employee who feels safe enough to be honest will provide you valuable information on other potential problems in the organization and will give you input on what changes you may need to make in order to become a better leader yourself.

working to improve. Seeking their advice lets them know that you are willing to help them, which creates an atmosphere of trust.

Leaders have a duty to set the tone with employees that they are allowed to honestly express their frustrations as well, without any fear of retaliation from you, as long as they do so with respect. An employee who feels safe enough to be honest will provide you valuable information on other potential problems in the organization and will give you input on what changes you may need to make in order to become a better leader yourself. I found that I grew the most as a leader when I was willing to ask my employees to give me honest feedback on areas they thought I could improve.

All of us want to be the best we can be, but none of us will get there if we don't help by giving honest feedback. Simply firing an employee without letting them know what they were doing wrong is such a disservice to them; without feedback, they will likely go on to the next company and repeat those same mistakes. Respect them enough to tell them how they can correct their behavior, so that they can go on to their next job with a higher chance for success. Remember that you are helping them by telling the truth. And if your voice shakes a little—well, that's okay—as long as you don't let it stop you from speaking the truth.

We all need people who will give us feedback. That is how we improve.

—*Bill Gates*

The only way any of us can know all of the areas we can improve on is if we are open to feedback from others. But the only way we will get the valuable feedback others have to give is if we create an atmosphere that allows others to be comfortable giving it.

Giving feedback to someone on areas needing improvement is already uncomfortable for the person who gives it. It's never fun to deliver news to someone that might cause them to be upset or feel badly. Too often people hold back giving anything but positive feedback to others, because they don't want to feel the level of discomfort that comes from offering suggestions on how to improve. But sadly, if people don't share those suggestions, the other person will miss out on the opportunity to improve and become the very best they can be.

That's why the onus lies on the shoulders of the person asking for feedback to create an atmosphere that lets people feel comfortable sharing it. They can do that by showing that they are truly open to suggestions by listening intently while the other person speaks and then really considering what the other person is saying, without jumping to conclusions or shutting them down.

The second the person seeking feedback gets defensive or cuts the other person off, the other person will shut down and not talk further, and thus the valuable feedback will not get heard and the ability to improve will be hindered. Not only will it shut down the person who was trying to give feedback, but it will make everyone else observing the situation also stop and think twice before opening their mouths with feedback, in fear that they too will be rejected—or even worse, made to feel disrespected. The chances of any valuable feedback coming forth in those scenarios becomes nil ... by that point, it just ain't gonna happen.

On the flip side, we can all appreciate that taking feedback from others is hard, especially if you are asking for feedback on something you have worked really hard on and have emotionally exhausted yourself with before you even begin asking for feedback. That's why all of us, before we ever ask for the feedback to be given, have to take an emotional step back and really gear ourselves up to be open to hearing what others are going to tell us. It might even take a little coach pep talk with yourself in the bathroom mirror before you walk into the meeting—look yourself in that mirror and go all Vince Lombardi-ish on yourself, saying, "We want this feedback. We need this feedback. We are going to go in there and show them that we are listening to their feedback and that we appreciate it, even if it hurts a little to hear it, because that is how we are going to ultimately become the best we can be. We can do this!!!" It may sound silly, but sometimes that's exactly the kind of thing we have to do to help ourselves get into the right frame of mind, and if doing it helps us to create the atmosphere that will generate feedback, then I say do it!

Ken Blanchard said, "Feedback is the breakfast of champions."[7] So if you want to enjoy the pancakes and eggs, invite people to the table, create an atmosphere that allows them to share, and truly enjoy the meal.

Receiving Feedback: Stop Defending, and Start Listening

To grow and improve is a desire that most of us share. Yet in order to grow and improve, we must first be willing to acknowledge our areas of weakness; we must accept who we are in order to become something better. So how can we best recognize our weaknesses? We can stop defending and start listening.

Feedback is the quickest way to learn about our weaknesses and those areas we most need to improve. Knowing our weaknesses is the most important step in overcoming them. Why then do people get defensive the moment they receive feedback that challenges or corrects them, if that is the very thing needed for them to improve?

7   Ken Blanchard, "Feedback is the Breakfast of Champions," Berrett-Koehler Publishers, accessed November 14, 2018, https://www.bkconnection.com/bkblog/ken-blanchard/feedback-is-the-breakfast-of-champions.

We have all heard the term "fight or flight" in describing what happens to someone when feeling physically threatened. When a person's views, ideas, or behaviors are threatened, especially when they have put significant time, effort, or money into them, there is a similar response, known as being "defensive." Any sugges-

Feedback is the quickest way to learn about our weaknesses and those areas we most need to improve.

tions that conflict with their idea or behavior can send a person into defensive mode. The person's nervous system begins to overheat, and their body becomes tense. In this state, they are unable to take in much new information, as they become solely focused on defending their position.

There are many different defensive strategies used when a person is feeling challenged, criticized, or corrected: They will deny, make excuses, challenge, rationalize, explain, justify, blame, avoid, withdraw, or go on the attack, to name a few. To a person on the defense, any new knowledge feels threatening, and they are unable to see any side but their own. Learning and growth become impossible when a person is defensive.

Given that our desire is to grow and improve, and given that we cannot grow when we are defensive, it is imperative to take steps to avoid this response.

- The most important element in avoiding it is to listen. Our ability to form healthy relationships with others in business, whether it be coworkers, advisors, board members, managers, or clients, is a direct result of our ability to listen well.

- Sometimes when hearing feedback, we must force ourselves to take a deep breath, or if necessary, ask to be excused for a moment so that we might step away and regain our composure. Then we can return with a clear head, ready to actively listen.

- It is important to note that when we are feeling tired or stressed out, we can react defensively without meaning to, so it's important to stay self-aware about how our emotions may be influencing our reactions during these times.

- Be careful not to expect everyone to see things exactly the way you do. One of the best things about diversity of thought is that it helps us to view things from different perspectives, so welcome the opportunity to expand your horizons. If, while receiving feedback, you are feeling attacked, feel comfortable to express that you are feeling that way in a calm and respectful tone. It may very well be that the other person isn't even aware that their tone is causing you to feel threatened, and your expressing your feelings might help them be more sensitive with their approach.

- As the other person is talking, look for areas you can agree with them. Finding areas of common agreement will help both parties to feel collaborative rather than combative.

- If you truly can't find any points to agree with, ask for specific examples—not in an accusatory way, but in a way to show that you genuinely desire to better understand their point of view by seeking examples that will help illustrate the problem more clearly for you.

- Be quick to apologize when you should. Doing so shows a tremendous amount of maturity and respect for the other person. It shows that you are willing to be accountable for your behavior and it demonstrates that you can be trusted to take responsibility for your actions.

- Stay on topic. Don't use the conversation as a way to start bringing up your own grievances that are unrelated to the current discussion—that is a destructive tactic that only manipulates you into believing that you are superior to the other person and therefore don't need to listen.

After hearing the other person out with an open mind, if you are still struggling with their point of view, simply thank them for sharing their views with you and let them know that you genuinely want to take time to ponder what they have said, stating that you will come back to them after you have given it more thought.

When someone is willing to take the time to give you constructive feedback, listen. Remember that truly confident people are able to listen respectfully to other perspectives, and then to genuinely consider and evaluate if there is truth in what others are saying. They are able to do all of this without feeling that other perspectives are in any way diminishing their own. Don't deny yourself the opportunity to learn. If you want to improve, stop defending and start listening.

Great Employees Are Not Replaceable.

One of the most important lessons I learned during my years as a CEO was that great employees are not replaceable. It isn't the technology or the product that makes a company great, it's the people. And companies who see their good employees as replaceable are wrong—good employees are not replaceable. Let me clarify what I mean by "replaceable." Can a company hire someone to fill a position to replace someone else? Of course they can. In today's market, the world is ripe with candidates who are eager and willing to take the job. But putting a behind in a seat doesn't replace a great employee. It simply puts a new behind in a seat.

Business leaders who adopt the attitude that anyone is replaceable, thinking they can simply hire someone with a greater skill set or someone with a more prestigious pedigree, are fooling themselves. When a company has a truly great employee, that employee carries value that simply cannot be replaced. They carry deep institutional knowledge of the organization. They have extensive product, systems, and process knowledge. They hold client relationships that have been built over many years. They carry tremendous experience on what has worked and what hasn't worked for the company in the past. And great employees have camaraderie and influence with their coworkers, which when lost has an impact on the corporate culture.

> **Business leaders who adopt the attitude that anyone is replaceable, thinking they can simply hire someone with a greater skill set or someone with a more prestigious pedigree, are fooling themselves.**

When a company loses a great employee, it gives other employees reason for pause, thinking, "Why would they leave the organization, and why would the organization let them get away? Is there something wrong with this company that I should be worried about? Maybe I should start looking elsewhere myself." Not only will other employees question it, but clients may question it as well. When clients trust an employee and that employee leaves, the clients begin to ask themselves the same questions as the employees: "Is there something wrong that I am unaware of? What might have caused that employee to leave? Should we be out looking for a new vendor?" The ripple effect of losing a great employee is tremendous, and it goes well beyond what is easily quantified.

Companies need to be very thoughtful when making decisions around compensation for their employees. To deny a reasonable increase to a top performer in the organization can be a very costly mistake. To try and hire a replacement for a great employee will inevitably cost the organization significantly more when they take into account the starting wage required in their attempt to "hire up"—not to mention the cost in time and money to train a replacement and get them up to full production, or the opportunity cost of having created a gap in the institutional knowledge of the business.

Obviously, there will be some life events that take great employees away from a company, which cannot be stopped. But when companies have the option to retain great employees, they should do everything in their power to do so. Companies that want to retain their top talent need to be willing to show them appreciation, compensate them well, and treat them with the respect they deserve. At the end of the day, it won't be a great product or service or technology that makes a company succeed—it is great people that make a great company. Appreciate those men and women who dedicate their time and talents each day to make your company a success, because those are the people who cannot be replaced.

A Little Appreciation Goes a Long Way.

A person who feels appreciated will always do more than what is expected. Appreciation is one of life's greatest motivators, so when we take the time to let people know that we value them, it inspires them to continue doing even more. That is precisely why gratitude is the gift that keeps on giving.

Francis Flynn, a professor of organizational behavior at Stanford, writes:[8]

> *Individuals often withhold help because they are uncertain about whether beneficiaries will appreciate their assistance. Expressions of gratitude can signify that a beneficiary values, needs, and accepts one's assistance. Previous research has shown that grateful feelings enable people to savor positive experiences, cope with stress, and strengthen social relationships. A disposition toward gratitude is also associated with higher levels of subjective well-being, demonstrating that counting one's blessings can increase positive emotions and health.*

He goes on to share that in a study published in the *Journal of Personality and Social Psychology*, researchers Adam Grant and Francesca Gino ran four experiments designed to look at how being

---

8   Francis J. Flynn, "Frank Flynn: Gratitude, the Gift That Keeps on Giving," Insights by Stanford Business, March 1, 2012, https://www.gsb.stanford.edu/insights/frank-flynn-gratitude-gift-keeps-giving.

thanked played into feelings of personal competence and the perception of being valued.[9]

In each of the four experiments, they tested having someone thank another person for their involvement, then studied the resulting behavior of the person who received the thanks. Each participant was measured on how effective they felt they were at the task as well as how valued they felt. The results were very telling:

The findings suggest that when helpers are thanked for their efforts, the resulting sense of being socially valued is critical in encouraging them to provide more help in the future. Gratitude expressions spill over onto other beneficiaries as well, suggesting that one can spark a chain of prosocial behavior with a simple thank-you. Overall, the research affirms our general intuition—that giving thanks can have important implications for encouraging actions that promote cooperation. Clearly, a little appreciation goes a long way.[10]

As a boss I found that the most powerful motivator for my employees was a simple note of thanks from their boss. And according to a survey performed by Glassdoor, that wasn't just true for my employees—it rings true for employees across the board. Their survey found that employees would stay longer at their companies and work much harder in their jobs if they felt more appreciated by their bosses.[11] Clearly, showing appreciation is just smart business!

---

9   Adam Grant and Francesca Gino, "A little thanks goes a long way: Explaining why gratitude expressions motivate prosocial behavior," *Journal of Personality and Social Psychology* 98, no. 6 (2010): 946-55, doi: 10.1037/a0017935.

10   Ibid.

11   "More Than Half Of Employees Would Stay Longer At Their Company If Bosses Showed More Appreciation, Glassdoor Survey," Glassdoor, November 13, 2013, https://www.glassdoor.com/about-us/employees-stay-longer-company-bosses-showed-appreciation-glassdoor-survey/.

There is no doubt that when we say the words "thank you," we make the other person feel important and valued, which raises their self-esteem and helps improve their self-image. In addition, saying "thank you" not only improves their self-esteem, it improves our own self-esteem as well. Each time we say those words to another person, we feel better about ourselves, our attitude improves, and we become more

Employees would stay longer at their companies and work much harder in their jobs if they felt more appreciated by their bosses.

grateful. This phenomenon is often referred to as the law of reciprocity, which says, "If you make me feel good about myself, I will find a way to make you feel good about yourself." That act of showing appreciation through something as simple as saying "thank you" ignites others to go the extra mile for us, and we in turn become inspired to go the extra mile for them. Thus we see how gratitude truly is the gift that keeps on giving.

PART IV

STAND OUT
AND STAY
STANDING

CHAPTER 10

BECOMING A GREAT EMPLOYEE

What It Takes to Be a Great Employee: The Parable of the Oranges

---

Being a great employee pays off with better positions, higher pay, and more frequent promotions. But some workers struggle to understand exactly what it takes to become a truly great employee.

One of the most important elements of having a successful company is having a workforce of great employees. That is why it is so important that leaders are able to explain things to employees in a way that can be easily understood and that creates a clear picture of what you are looking for.

The best explanation of how one becomes a great employee can be seen through a simple story known as the Parable of the Oranges.[12]

THE PARABLE OF THE ORANGES

There was a young man who had ambitions to work for a company because it paid very well and was very prestigious. He prepared his résumé and had several interviews. Eventually, he was given an entry-level position. Then he turned his ambition to his next goal—a supervisor position that would afford him even greater prestige and more pay. So he completed the tasks he was given. He came in early some mornings and stayed late so the boss would see him putting in long hours.

After five years a supervisor position became available. But, to the young man's great dismay, another employee, who had only worked for the company for six months, was given the promotion. The young man was very angry, and he went to his boss and demanded an explanation.

The wise boss said, "Before I answer your questions, would you do a favor for me?"

"Yes, sure," said the employee.

"Would you go to the store and buy some oranges? My

12   Randall L. Ridd, "Living with a Purpose: The Importance of Real Intent," (lecture, Brigham Young University-Idaho, January 11, 2015).

wife needs them."

The young man agreed and went to the store. When he returned, the boss asked, "What kind of oranges did you buy?"

"I don't know," the young man answered. "You just said to buy oranges, and these are oranges. Here they are."

"How much did they cost?" the boss asked.

"Well, I'm not sure," was the reply. "You gave me $30. Here is your receipt, and here is your change."

"Thank you," said the boss. "Now, please have a seat and pay careful attention."

Then the boss called in the employee who had received the promotion and asked him to do the same job. He readily agreed and went to the store.

When he returned, the boss asked, "What kind of oranges did you buy?"

"Well," he replied, "the store had many varieties—there were navel oranges, Valencia oranges, blood oranges, tangerines, and many others, and I didn't know which kind to buy. But I remembered you said your wife needed the oranges, so I called her. She said she was having a party and that she was going to make orange juice. So I asked the grocer which of all these oranges would make the best orange juice. He said the Valencia orange was full of very sweet juice, so that's what I bought. I dropped them by your home on my way back to the office. Your wife was very pleased."

"How much did they cost?" the boss asked.

"Well, that was another problem. I didn't know how many to buy, so I once again called your wife and asked her how many guests she was expecting. She said twenty. I asked the grocer how many oranges would be needed to make juice for twenty people, and it was a lot. So, I asked the grocer if he could give me a quantity discount, and he did! These oranges normally cost seventy-five cents each, but I paid only fifty cents. Here is your change and the receipt."

The boss smiled and said, "Thank you; you may go."

He looked over at the young man who had been watching. The young man stood up, slumped his shoulders and said, "I see what you mean," as he walked dejectedly out of the office.

What was the difference between these two young men? They were both asked to buy oranges, and they did. You might say that one went the extra mile, or one was more efficient, or one paid more attention to detail. But the most important difference had to do with real intent rather than just going through the motions. The first young man was motivated by money, position, and prestige. The second young man was driven by an intense desire to please his employer and an inner commitment to be the best employee he could possibly be—and the outcome was obvious.

Anyone can be a great employee if that is their real intent. But real intent must come from within. It doesn't come from external motivators such as money or titles. Real intent comes from a genuine desire to do the right thing for the right reason along with an inner commitment to always put forth a best effort in all that one does. Great employees are willing to focus on helping others become more successful, and inevitably they themselves grow to become great leaders in the process. They take accountability for their actions and they own their mistakes. They gain reputations of being trustworthy, and they earn the respect of their coworkers. And they understand the value of a team.

> **Great employees are willing to focus on helping others become more successful, and inevitably they themselves grow to become great leaders in the process.**

I have always found that the best way to get what you want is to help others to get what they want. By helping your boss become more successful, you will inevitably become more successful yourself. And that is exactly what great employees do.

An Employee That Any Boss Would Be Thrilled to Hire

As a child, I was taught the importance of respect. We were taught to show respect for other people, show respect for others' cultures, show respect for people's position of authority, show respect for a venue, show respect for an event, and so on. This principle was greatly emphasized in my home, and it is something I have grown to value deeply. It has been a tremendous benefit to me in my business life and in my personal life. It has also allowed me to be comfortable mingling in any situation and with any group of people, even at times when situations have been extremely intimidating for me, because I knew that I would do okay so long as I applied the principles of respect that my parents taught me. From those experiences, I have come to understand that being able to respect others helps you have more confidence in yourself in every situation.

Trying to teach the importance of respect to other people, especially our own children ... well, these days it has become a bit more difficult. Especially when our children are being raised in a generation where respect has either not been taught, or if it has, it is not at all emphasized. Disrespect for elders, positions of authority, venues, cultures, events, and so on are all too widely accepted by young people. And as parents, when you try to correct and teach them, you typically get eye rolling and a, "You're just old school and don't get it" response. The frightening fact is that our kids are growing up in a generation where entitlement is the norm and respect is not.

The saddest part is that kids who don't learn respect as they are growing up end up entering the workforce only to get a rude awakening to the fact that success in the business world requires respect. Having respect in business requires that a person have respect for a boss, respect for a manager, respect for the company dress code, respect for being on time, respect for following through with commitments, respect for the values of the company, respect for the clients, respect for different cultures, respect for the work environment, respect for meetings and events, and the list goes on and on. Respect is essential if one desires to find any level of true success in business.

When a child is taught to act with respect in their home, and they choose to implement those teachings, they will be prepared to act with respect in the business world. If young people want to know what respect looks like, consider the following tips for how they show respect to their parents:

- **Be polite:** Put down your cell phone and look your parents in the eye. Smile. Say hello. Say thank you. Say excuse me. Say I'm sorry. Be on time. Follow through when you make a commitment.

- **Don't:** Don't roll your eyes or make rude comments under your breath. Don't trash your parents behind their backs. Don't raise your voice and storm off. Don't dig your heels in. Don't complain. Don't ignore.

- **Communicate:** Hold conversations with your parents. Open up and share your problems, your fears, your worries. Ask for their advice and input. Share your goals and your achievements with them.

- **Listen:** Realize that your parents have tremendous life experience, and chances are they have been exactly where you are before and can give you advice on how to weather the storms and avoid the pitfalls. Value their input. Don't let pride get in the way of listening and learning from those who have the knowledge to help you.

- **Be grateful:** Notice everything your parents do for you. Appreciate the sacrifices they make on your behalf. Don't take them for granted. Voice your appreciation on a regular basis.

Be willing to go the extra mile for them. Keep in mind that they want what is best for you and they want you to succeed.

Every single one of these tips on how to respect parents can be applied directly toward how one should show respect in the business world. And I can tell you this—you show me a kid who treats their parents that way and I will show you an employee that any boss would be thrilled to hire.

Five Ways to Get a Promotion

Job security is something everyone longs for, and typically we view moving up in the organization as a sign that our jobs are indeed secure. Increased wealth and opportunity are also things we long for, and a promotion at work can help to achieve that. But receiving a promotion doesn't always come easily, so here are five suggestions to help in your efforts:

1. **Overachieve in your current position:** The first thing a boss will ask themselves when trying to decide whom to promote is, "How are they doing at the job they are currently assigned?" If a promotion is what you want, you first need to overachieve in your current position. Arrive a few minutes early each day and stay a few minutes late. Go the extra mile with every responsibility you take on. Even when you are asked to do something silly or seemingly unimportant, treat it with the utmost care and knock it out of the park. It will make

an impression as they are looking for people to entrust with further responsibility.

2. **Express your desire to move up:** It's important to make sure that people in management know that you want to move up. Let them know what your career goals are. Don't just share them once, share them multiple times so that they won't forget. If they don't know you are looking to move up, it is easy for them to assume that no one internally is interested in filling an open position and look elsewhere. There were employees who reached out to me as CEO to let me know of their desire to move up, and even if I didn't think they were ready yet, their names stood out in my mind every time a position would become available, until eventually I felt they were ready to be promoted.

3. **Seek and implement feedback:** If you are ever considered for a promotion and are ultimately not chosen, ask the people who interviewed you to give you feedback about why you were not selected. Ask what you can do going forward to have a better chance of being selected the next time a promotion becomes available. Then, when they give you feedback on how to change—DO IT. Implement the feedback you are given on how you can improve, and do it continuously. Nothing will frustrate a manager more than when they give an employee their feedback and the employee appears to be making changes for the first day or two only to go right back to the way they were before. If you desire to be promoted, you have to make the necessary changes in your behavior and make them permanent.

4. **Be a positive, uplifting person:** That alone will definitely get you noticed and make people want to work with you. Help the

people around you. Don't try to hold others back. Remember that if you can't be replaced, you can't be promoted. Be willing

The best team lead is one who has had the most members of their team go on to become team leads themselves. Leaders are people who grow other leaders.

to teach others to do everything you know how to do. The way a good leader is identified is by observing how many employees they have helped to escalate beyond themselves. For example, the best team lead is one who has had the most members of their team go on

to become team leads themselves. Leaders are people who grow other leaders. Be that person.

5. **Be accountable, be reliable, and be completely trustworthy:** Go the extra mile to learn everything you can, even if it's not part of your job. Ask "Why?" Understand the "why" behind what you do at your company, not just the "what." A doer learns the what, but a leader understands the why. So learn why.

6. **Set your goals and then work your tail off to make them happen.** Opportunities for promotions are endless, whether within your own organization or in a new one. Don't get discouraged if it takes longer than you would like. It may be that you just aren't ready yet. And don't give up the first time a promotion passes you by. Look at each failed promotion as an opportunity to learn and improve. If you keep your attitude positive, your work ethic strong, and your desires known, eventually an opportunity will arise that is perfect for you. Ask for it!

Put Yourself in the Running. You May Not Get Chosen, but You Will Get Noticed.

If there is something you want badly enough, my advice is this: put yourself in the running. Even if you don't get chosen, you will get noticed.

I was constantly looking for great people to fill management positions within the company. Even though growth is a huge blessing for a company, it can also be a challenge, because it requires you to find and recruit all the right people to help you manage that growth. My personal preference was always to look within our organization before branching out to fill positions, and so with each new opening we would try to post it internally before advertising externally.

On one particular occasion, a position was posted for a high-level management position, the head of a department in the company. The day after it was posted, I received an email from an employee whose name didn't ring a bell, letting me know that he would like to be considered for the position. I gathered a few members of my executive team and asked them to tell me about this young man; I would have expected to recognize the name if he had been on our short list of internal people we felt were qualified for the position. When I shared his name, they too were surprised—he wasn't someone who had ever held a position of management within the company, so it was a surprise that he would have the courage to throw his name in the ring for such a high-ranking position as head of the department.

In the end, this employee was not chosen for the management position, because at that point he lacked experience. However, something else amazing happened. Because this young man had the courage to throw his name in the ring, from that point forward he got noticed. We now knew who he was, and his name came to mind every time a new position became available in the company. And sure enough, once he gained more management experience, he was eventually promoted to head of the department—the very position he had tried for early on. It may have taken him a little time to get there, but chances are he never would have gotten there, and certainly not as soon as he did, if he hadn't initially stepped up and put himself in the running.

From that point forward he got noticed. We now knew who he was, and his name came to mind every time a new position became available in the company.

Too many people are afraid of putting themselves in the running. They are afraid that if they do and then don't get chosen they will end up worse off than they were to begin with. That is simply NOT TRUE! There is absolutely no shame in trying, even if you don't succeed. There is only shame in not making the attempt, because if you don't make the attempt you will never get anywhere in life. Never hold yourself back from throwing your hat in the ring over fear of not being chosen, because I guarantee that even if you don't get chosen, you will definitely get noticed, and that is all it takes to set you on a path toward accomplishing everything you ever dreamed of.

CHAPTER 11

AVOIDING SELF-SABOTAGE

Check Yourself Before You Wreck Yourself.

Just think how much you'd get done if you stopped actively sabotaging your own work.

—Seth Godin

I was standing in the security line at an airport when a TSA worker came walking alongside the line, yelling out in an animated way, "No liquids, no aerosols, no gels or creams on the airplane … You better check yourself before you wreck yourself!" I couldn't stop myself from laughing out loud, imagining what it would be like if every CEO walked through the halls of their company yelling out something similar—"No negativity, no dishonesty, no disrespect in the workplace … You better check yourself before you wreck yourself!" Frankly, it might actually be a good idea. After all, that TSA worker certainly got every one of us standing in line that day to think twice about what we had in our carry-ons.

Whether it's procrastination, acting impulsively, laziness, over-committing, overthinking, self-pity, giving up, or just being negative, everyone has engaged in some form of self-sabotage at one point or another in their work life. That is why it is so critical that you stop and ask yourself if you are engaging in self-sabotage when it comes to your job. Is it possible that you may be the very person standing in the way of your own success? Let's look at ways one might wreck themselves at work:

- Having a bad attitude, a negative attitude, or a sassy attitude.

- Getting defensive when management is giving you feedback on how you need to improve.

- Hanging out with negative people in the office.

- Contributing to or participating in negative situations.

- Gossiping with coworkers.

- Going to lunch with coworkers in order to bash the company or your managers.

- Sharing with coworkers when you have gotten in trouble for poor performance or poor attitude rather than keeping it confidential and fixing your bad behavior.

- Discussing salary with coworkers or inappropriately sharing confidential HR information.

- Going against a company policy.

- Not living the company values.

- Not taking the time to read all communication from company leadership.

- Pretending to be working when the boss or a manager walks by.

- Suddenly changing the subject as a manager walks by to hide an inappropriate conversation.

- Lying to your manager.

- Lying to anyone.

- Treating others disrespectfully.

- Having an attitude of entitlement.

- Acting as though you are better than other people or other people are less than you.

- Not giving an honest day's work for an honest day's pay.

Let's look at some steps that can help one avoid self-sabotage in the workplace:

- Be self-aware. Go through the list of examples above and be honest with yourself about which things you have been guilty of doing.

- Accept responsibility. Admit to yourself that you are the one in control of your own behavior and acknowledge that you have the ability to change it.

- Stop making excuses and stop justifying the bad choices you have been making. Stop convincing yourself that you are justified to do these things that are sabotaging your success in the workplace.

- Find a strong support system. Find trusted coworkers who are willing to help you stay on the right track. Your best bet is a manager or a leader, because they have a vested interest in helping you succeed. After all, the best leaders rate themselves by the success of the people they lead.

- Spread positivity. Become known for being the person who always looks for the positive in every situation. Lift and encourage your coworkers. Always speak positively about the company and its leadership. If there are things you have been unhappy with in the past find positive ways to help improve them. You will have the greatest influence and impact when you point out possible solutions in a positive way.

Remind yourself of all those self-sabotaging behaviors you can't be taking with you into the building.

- Live with integrity. Give an honest day's work every single day. Be truthful with everyone. Do what you say you will do. Give open feedback in a respectful way. Be trustworthy and dependable.

"Check yourself before you wreck yourself" isn't just something you should do one time. Just like you have to clear TSA security each time you go to the airport, you should take the time to "check yourself before you wreck yourself" as you walk through the doors to enter your office building each day. Remind yourself of all those self-sabotaging behaviors you can't be taking with you into the building. And just as the TSA security rules are there to make sure you have a safe flight, the steps for avoiding self-sabotage are there to make sure you reach the height of success.

The moment you take responsibility for everything in your life is the moment you can change anything in your life.

—Hal Elrod

Passive-Aggressive Behavior Will Destroy a Company's Culture.

Passive-aggressive behavior in any company is a cancer to the culture, and can end up killing both a great company and the self-esteem of the individuals working there. For anyone wondering what passive-aggressive behavior looks like, here are some examples that paint a picture.

A passive-aggressive person is someone who:
- appears to be agreeable and supportive on the surface, but behind the scenes will backstab, undercut, and sabotage;
- constantly states that you can trust their words when their actions have consistently shown that not to be true;

- makes promises about things when they have no intention of following through, often then blaming things that were "out of their control" for preventing them from fulfilling their promise;

- smiles and agrees with you to your face, but then disagrees or even sabotages things behind your back;

- states, "I was supportive of you, but this other person wasn't, so there was nothing I could do," to place blame on someone else rather than voicing their own lack of support for the matter;

- gives positive praise and feedback to you directly, but then takes actions to undercut you to coworkers and management;

- withholds important information from other employees in order to make themselves appear more important and more valuable and in an attempt to make others around them fail;

- uses sarcasm or humor to make fun of someone else so that they can hide behind an "I was just kidding" attitude, when actually they meant every word; and

- wants everyone to believe that they are their biggest supporter and advocate, refusing to be honest and direct about their true feelings.

I observed a company where passive-aggressive behavior was rapidly becoming embedded in the culture. The behavior appeared to initially stem from several members of upper management, and it quickly began to permeate throughout all levels of the company. As employees observed their coworkers getting rewarded for passive-aggressive behavior, they either took the "If you can't beat 'em, join 'em" road or they began seeking employment opportunities elsewhere to escape the toxic environment. As the toxic behavior spread, employees started becoming depressed and despondent. What had once been a company that employees were excited to be a part of became nothing more than a paycheck they would collect until something better came along. Observing this cancer as it spread through the organization was unbelievably painful, especially as I watched the impact to those great individuals who were trying desperately to "hang in there" out of loyalty to their clients and loyalty to the business they once loved.

> **What had once been a company that employees were excited to be a part of became nothing more than a paycheck they would collect until something better came along.**

So why would any company tolerate this type of behavior? Why would any leader allow such destructive, dishonest behavior from the people they lead? The sad fact is that, in large organizations, too often the leader becomes busy and disconnected as to what is happening under their watch. Some leaders even adopt the "I don't really want to know" attitude, because they are already feeling overwhelmed themselves, and knowing about it would mean they have a responsibility to fix it. Other leaders may be surrounded by an entire team of passive-aggressive executives who tell them everything is great even when it's not. These executives always have someone they can offer as a sacrificial lamb when something goes wrong, making it appear as though all that is needed to rectify the problem is to fire the worker and all will be well in the world.

When a CEO is surrounded by top executives who are passive-aggressive, it becomes necessary to set aside the words they hear from these people and instead observe their actions and the actions of the people reporting to them. Words from the mouth of a passive-aggressive manager cannot be trusted, as they will always tell the CEO what the CEO wants to hear, and they will always paint the picture of having everything perfectly under control. In this environment, it becomes necessary for the CEO to be willing to take a closer look at things to find a way that allows employees at every level to share their concerns about leadership without fear of retaliation. Short of that, a CEO will remain clueless until the problems become so great that even the strongest of companies will implode.

Employees dealing with passive-aggressive leaders need to find a way to bring it to the attention of their CEO. Unless a CEO becomes aware of the problem, they likely won't fix it. I recognize that this may feel like a big risk to an employee, but quite frankly, the bigger risk is allowing your future career to be dictated by someone whose behavior has proven that they cannot be trusted.

Honesty with respect is always the best policy, in life and in the workplace. Voicing your opinions, if done in a respectful way, is always positive and should be welcomed, encouraged, and even rewarded. Don't allow passive-aggressive behavior to exist in your company. If it exists today, change it. Remove those people who perpetuate the behavior, starting with those in leadership positions, and send the message that this behavior will not be tolerated. Life is too short to have misery in the workplace, and the price is too great for the business and for the people involved. Create a culture of integrity, honesty, and respect. Create a culture you can be proud of.

Being the Best Isn't About Knowing the Most.

The greatest enemy of knowledge is not ignorance, it is the illusion of knowledge.

—Stephen Hawking

When an individual believes they know all the answers, they shut themselves off from the possibility that there is more they might learn on a subject. They limit themselves from experiencing personal growth and gaining intelligence.

Such an individual is commonly referred to as a know-it-all. In a work setting, the know-it-all can be one of the most dangerous types of employee, and in a leadership position, they can be the kiss of death for a company.

There is a tremendous difference between a confident person and a know-it-all.

A confident person is open to the reality that there is always new knowledge to be gained. They are open to hearing others' opinions and ideas, because they recognize that those opinions pose no threat to their own status of being intelligent. They listen with an open mind and consider whether any of this new information can open their eyes to new ideas and thoughts. As a result, they will continuously learn and grow in their intelligence.

Know-it-alls view others' opinions as a threat. They immediately jump into a defensive mode of explaining why this new information is invalid and why their knowledge is superior. They typically reject any idea that was not their own, and they relish the opportunity to point out the failures of others that they feel could have been avoided if people had just listened to them.

I have seen firsthand the impact an office know-it-all can have on their coworkers, and it is not good. In a group setting, the employees who are already hesitant to share ideas will shut down almost completely when working with a know-it-all, thus cutting off any flow of new ideas and differing perspectives. Confident employees who genuinely add value to the organization will stand up to a know-it-all for a while, but eventually they will grow tired of the constant battle to be heard and will seek employment elsewhere. And employees who are good worker bees will typically stay quiet and just let the know-it-all have the limelight, but they will often keep their ideas and opinions to themselves, allowing the know-it-all to dictate and drive everything. In each situation, the company suffers.

The most difficult situation for a manager when the know-it-all actually has great talents they bring to the company. As a leader, you appreciate their gifts and see the value those gifts can add to the organization. But a good leader cannot overlook the impact that the gifted employee is having on the rest of the organization. A good leader cannot get sucked into the mind-set of thinking that the talents of one employee are more important than the morale of many employees. As painful as losing a talented person can be, it is more painful to negatively impact the entire culture of a company by supporting the "all-about-me" attitude of a single employee.

Having gone through these scenarios myself as a CEO, I know firsthand how difficult it can be to have to terminate someone who is truly gifted. But I also know firsthand the benefit to morale when the rest of the company sees that their leader wasn't willing to value one person's talent over anyone else's. It is critical that leaders send a clear message that everyone matters equally to the organization, regardless of their title or position.

None of us are immune from having to deal with a know-it-all at one point or another in the workplace. And if we are not careful ourselves, we run the risk of becoming that person. Here are a few thoughts that might help with both situations.

It is critical that leaders send a clear message that everyone matters equally to the organization, regardless of their title or position.

How to Deal With a Know-It-All in the Workplace

- Don't engage in confrontation with a know-it-all. Confrontation only ignites their insecurities and sets them into defensive mode. You cannot win a battle with a know-it-all, because in their own mind they are incapable of being wrong, no matter how much evidence you present to the contrary. Rather than disputing them, try an approach of hearing them out and then stating, "I can see why you have come to that conclusion. What would your solution be if [insert a fact here] was added to the equation needing to be solved?" By acknowledging their initial answer as correct and then adding a new fact for their consideration, you are first validating their current intelligence and then giving them an opening to change their opinion without them having to admit to being wrong in their initial answer. In essence, you are asking them a new question based on the new fact, allowing them to come up with an answer to an even harder question and giving them an opportunity to showcase their intelligence at an even higher level.

- Don't try to change a know-it-all. They didn't become a know-it-all overnight; that came from years of deep insecurities that have grown over time. Believing that you can somehow change them will only lead to further frustration. Instead, recognize that their arrogance is simply a mask for their insecurities, and allow your compassion for their lack of confidence help you be patient and kind with them. Be grateful that you don't carry the burden of those insecurities yourself.

- Be willing to compliment the know-it-all for the special talents they bring to the table. Sometimes our natural response to a know-it-all is to pull back and not give them any compliments, believing that compliments will only serve to "feed the beast." But that belief is false. Giving a know-it-all genuine and sincere compliments regarding their gifts and talents will help to counteract their belief that they are not good enough, which is at the root of their self-esteem issues. Be willing to give them credit where credit is due.

How to Ensure That You Don't Become a Know-It-All Yourself

- Have the desire to continuously learn new things, and always stay humble enough to be teachable. A constant desire to learn and grow will help you stay in the right mind-set.

- When you are having a discussion on a topic you feel confident in, feel free to share your thoughts on the matter, but always close by saying, "Those are my initial thoughts, but I would really value hearing your thoughts as well." This confirms to the other person that you value their ideas and lets them know that you are open to expanding your own view.

- Never feel threatened by others' opinions and ideas. Rather, see them as opportunities to expand your way of thinking and to learn something you may not have considered before. Encourage others to share their knowledge with you, and be eager to listen and absorb new information. Be generous in giving genuine compliments to others about their knowledge and ideas. Your willingness to appreciate them will help you avoid becoming defensive or feeling threatened in any way.

Being the best isn't about knowing the most. Being the best is about confidently admitting you don't know it all, while embracing every opportunity to learn and grow from the wisdom of others. Have confidence in your ability to learn, not in the amount of information you already know. Always remember that wisdom comes from gaining knowledge and experience over the course of time—not in a day or a week, but over a lifetime, so never stop learning.

Never feel threatened by others' opinions and ideas. Rather, see them as opportunities to expand your way of thinking and to learn something you may not have considered before.

Coping in a Toxic Work Environment

It is your reaction to adversity, not the adversity itself, that determines how your life story will develop.

—Dieter F. Uchtdorf.

I had the occasion to observe a group of employees who were working in a toxic work environment. I witnessed the decline of self-esteem in each of them as they endured month after month of poor leadership and dysfunction in their workplace. I was truly amazed at the change in countenance of these employees as their situation grew worse. If one could have taken a "before" photo of these employees prior to their being in a toxic environment and an "after" photo when they were months into it, the physical manifestations of the negativity they endured would be staggering. Slowly, I observed each of these employees reach their breaking point and one by one resign from the company. Each of them had good paying jobs with fabulous benefits, but the toxicity they dealt with each day was so unbearable that no amount of money would have made it worth the cost to their well-being.

They left their jobs without having new jobs lined up, because they'd reached a point where they recognized that the toll that the toxic environment was taking had become far too great to stay another day.

You may not be in such an extremely toxic work environment that you are willing to quit your job before having secured a new one, but most people will have the occasion to deal with some level of toxicity in the workplace, so here are a few tips on how to cope with it when it occurs:

- I believe the most important thing to recognize when working in a toxic environment is that it is *not* a reflection of who you truly are. Oftentimes in a toxic workplace, there is an abundance of tearing others down, passive-aggressive leadership, destructive gossip, conniving politics, and rampant negativity. When you are surrounded by this daily, it can really start to affect your sense of self-worth. It is imperative that you learn to separate the negativity you are swimming in every day from the reality of who you truly are. This demoralizing effect is the biggest danger in staying long term in any toxic environment, and to combat this you will have to find ways to remind yourself daily that you are not a reflection of your current surroundings. Placing positive and uplifting quotes on the wall of your office or cubicle that will help keep your spirits up can be very helpful. Also, taking time out daily for a short walk by yourself is a great way to detach and allow for positive self-talk to remind yourself of the qualities you possess that make you amazing. It's important to remind yourself who you truly are.

- Another important coping step is to realize that you cannot control what other people say and do; you can only control your own actions and reactions. The sooner you accept that, the better for your own mental well-being. This realization allows you to let go of owning other people's negative behavior and empowers you to focus on improving yourself.

The more you can focus on improving yourself in a negative environment, the better, because when you finally get the opportunity to escape the situation you are in, you take all that personal growth along with you.

• Finally, try to focus on turning your bad situation into a good learning experience. Most often, our strongest personal growth comes from living through our most difficult situations. When you are working in a toxic environment, pay close attention to the lessons you can take away from the experience. Perhaps you can learn the qualities in a leader that you never want to emulate. Perhaps you can learn management's mistakes that you would not want to repeat if the opportunity for management ever comes your way. In every bad situation, there is something you can learn that will help you become a better person, so focus on each lesson you are learning.

As difficult as a toxic work environment may be, never allow yourself to become less than who you are meant to be out of anger or spite for your current employer. Always conduct yourself with integrity and always put in your very best effort toward the job you were hired to do. It's easy to fall into the trap of giving up on the job, but the bottom line is that as long as you are taking a paycheck you have an obligation to give an honest day's work. Don't allow yourself to justify personal bad behavior on the failures that exist in your company's leadership. At times, it may feel like the only option in a toxic situation is to fight back, but the reality is that doing so only hurts your integrity. Know that your

Most often, our strongest personal growth comes from living through our most difficult situations.

reputation will continue far beyond the company you are with today, and nothing is worth trading your integrity for. Do your absolute best every day at your job, and the word will get out to other companies of your impeccable character and strong work ethic. People talk far more in the business world than you may realize, and the word of your positive or negative behavior will spread farther and wider than you may think, so never do anything you need be ashamed of.

Continue to search diligently for a better work environment to switch to, and be sure to let others know that you are interested in new opportunities for work. Then give your very best at work up to the very day you joyfully hand in your resignation letter and move on to bigger, better, and happier things.

You Hate Your Job but You're Scared to Quit

You wake up every morning miserable because you can't stand the thought of going to a job you hate. You moan and groan so much about it that not only are you miserable, but everyone around you is as well. You get through each day of misery only to go home to bed so that you can revisit it all over again tomorrow. If you hate your job so much, then why stay? The answer is simple—change is scary. You hate your job, but you're scared to quit.

You have to ask yourself what is more frightening—the thought of being miserable day after day at a job you hate, or the thought of a job unknown?

People tell themselves that "the devil you know is better than the devil you don't." Sure, they may be miserable and unhappy now, but what if a new job makes them even more miserable and unhappy? And yes, their boss may be a jerk, but at least they know the extent of the current boss's jerkiness. And at least they know they aren't getting fired from their current job, but with a new company, who knows if they'll get fired, leaving them with no job at all. They have success-fully convinced themselves that the unknown is far worse than their current situation.

Now stop and consider an alternative view. What if a new job turns out to be awesome? What if your new boss actually cares about helping you succeed? What if the new company values your skills and talents, and even rewards you for them? What if it meant you'd wake up happy and excited to go do a job you love every day? What if *that* is the descrip-tion of the unknown? The fact is that you will never know which is better until you decide to make a choice. As I see it, there are only two options. You can either (a) change your circumstance by finding a new job, or (b) change your attitude about your current job. If you decide that you want to seek out a new job, here are five recommendations to consider:

What if a new job turns out to be awesome? What if your new boss actually cares about helping you succeed? What if the new company values your skills and talents, and even rewards you for them?

1. It's easier to get hired by a new company while you are still employed by your current one. New employers like it when you are currently employed, because it says that another company values you enough to keep you on board. It also lets the new employer feel that by hiring you away, they are winning a

competition with your current employer. So, try to find a new job before you quit the current one.

2.   Make a list of the things in your current job that influence your feelings of misery. Is it the duties you perform, the people you work with, the industry you're in? Figure out what you dislike so that you can seek out companies that differ in those key areas.

3.   Make a list of the people you know who might have leads about new jobs. Networking will almost always be your best option for finding a new job. Often you may even work with a vendor or a customer who might make an excellent new employer for you, so consider every avenue.

4.   Money should not be your primary driver as you consider new jobs. Taking a lower-paying job that allows you to be happier may be worth doing. In my experience, the happier you are, the better you do, and the more you end up being rewarded for that down the road. So don't let a starting salary stop you from taking a position you love if there is room for that position to grow.

5.   Once your decision to find new employment is made, you will find yourself noticing opportunities all around you. You will find yourself looking for potential leads from every conversation you have. You will begin to attend events that you previously found boring, because those events now represent the possibility of finding something new. Simply making the decision to find a new job opens your mind up to the field of potential, and you will quickly find your energy returning and your happiness level going up.

Don't allow your fear of the unknown to keep you from what you really want to do in life. Sure, you know exactly what you have today, but recognize that what lies in the unknown may very well be everything you ever hoped for. There is only one way to find out.

PART V

FINDING FULFILLMENT

CHAPTER 12

ACHIEVING BALANCE

Work-Life Balance: The Ultimate Oxymoron

One of the questions I am asked the most is "How do you do it? How do you balance work life and home life?" The honest answer is "I don't."

I don't do it all. No one can. For years, I battled the guilt of not being able to do it all, especially during the period of my life when I was a single working mom trying to also be a good CEO of a company that was growing quickly.

The very word "balance" caused me tremendous stress, because it felt like an unattainable dream that I would never be able to achieve. Then take that stress and add guilt—oh, the guilt. All working parents have the added burden of never-ending guilt. When you are at work, you feel guilty for not being at home. When you are at home, you feel guilty for not being at work. So basically you live in a twenty-four-hour guilt cycle that never ends, until

Rather than constantly feeling guilty and stressed in your pursuit of balance, turn your focus toward doing the very best you can do every day with the time you have.

one day when you finally accept the fact that you will never be able to do it all—but that is okay! It's not about doing it all, it's about doing the best you can with what you've got. So, rather than constantly feeling guilty and stressed in your pursuit of balance, turn your focus toward doing the very best you can do every day with the time you have. Here are five ideas to help you bring a little better balance into your life.

1. **Schedule down time.** An uncle who was also an entrepreneur told me when I started my very first business that I needed to block out time on my calendar for my family up front or I would never have time open. He was right, but unfortunately it took me a lot of years to realize how right he was. I never blocked out the family time, and work slowly overtook my life because I wasn't doing anything to schedule family time the same as I did business meetings. I would block off an hour lunch meeting with someone for business, so why not block off an hour dinner with my family at night?

It took me years and many hard lessons to figure out how critical it was for me to schedule my family time as carefully as I schedule my work day. The important thing is that you treat your family as if they matter just as much as the most important businessperson in the world (because they do!), and don't miss your scheduled meetings with them. Block out dinner on your calendar. Block out Saturday family events. Always keep Sunday as a sacred time with your family. Block out date night if you are married. Block out a once-a-month father/daughter or mother/son date with your child. Put these things on your calendar in advance of each month and then treat them with the same respect and consideration as you would any other meeting. Schedule that time with your family. They need you.

2. **Cut out the things that don't add value to your life.** There are a lot of things we waste time on in life—television, internet, video games, to name a few. I know because I am as guilty as many of you in allowing these things to overtake my family time. Cut it out! That is my advice. I have to remind myself of this often when I find myself on a Saturday looking at a cute pair of shoes

    If you have distractions in your life that take too much time away from family, put stickers on the TV or computer or video game console asking "What matters most in my life?"

    on Zappos when I could be out playing with my daughter. If you have distractions in your life that take too much time away from family, put stickers on the TV or computer or video game console asking "What matters most in my life?" It won't take long for that to hit you in the gut. Trust me. I have tried it. It's a good way to pull yourself away from wasting time when you could be spending it on quality time with your family.

3. **Avoid negative people that suck your energy.** People in your life who gossip, are negative, complain, or vent can be a huge drain on your energy. Avoid them! They will take up your time and leave absolutely no redeeming value in your universe. Don't give them two seconds of your day, because if you give two seconds they will take two hours. If you run into one of them, or they text you, Facebook message you, call you, or whatever, just don't engage. Simply tell them you are too busy being happy to swim in their pool of negativity, and then avoid them like the plague.

4. **Outsource those tasks that you can.** The day I discovered online grocery shopping was a very good day. Getting groceries was a tough task, especially when I was a single mom, so when I found out I could order groceries online and for a few dollars have them delivered to my front door I was thrilled. A few dollars saved me hours of time in a store. There are a lot of other, similar little things that can free up your day so that you can have more time with your family. Some other good finds are local dairies that deliver milk to your home, and dry cleaning services where you bring your clothes to the office and they pick them up for you.

5. **Take five for you.** In all the talk about work-life balance, we forget that part of balance is taking time for yourself. That is always the very first thing to go—you. Women are especially bad at this. We are so worried about everyone else that we forget about us. Everyone—men and women—needs a little time each day just for them, even if it's just five minutes. Time

to read a little, time to take a hot bath once in a while, time to swing on a swing and look at the garden. No matter what you choose to do with your five minutes, it needs to be time that is just for you. Meditate. Write in a journal. Pray. Just take that time for you—it will make you a better person for the ones you love, trust me.

I hope these ideas will help. The topic of balance is one I have struggled with my entire life, and I certainly haven't figured it out yet. But I am getting a little better at it all the time, and that is what is important.

Slow Down, Rest Up, Replenish, and Refill.

Fatigue is the common enemy of us all—so slow down, rest up, replenish, and refill.

—Jeffrey R. Holland

I have always had an incredible drive to work hard. When I am at work, I genuinely work my tail off. I am motivated and driven and focused on getting a tremendous amount done, and all of that is positive, but my problem lies in that I often don't know how to put things down and stop working for the night. There is always one more email, one more phone call, one more contract to review, one more issue to fix ... and the list goes on and on and on. Often it's so late at night when I finish working that I only have time to eat a late meal and go right to bed, only to wake up early the next morning and start over again. I get so busy with being busy that I forget the importance of balance. I forget the need to sometimes step back, take a deep breath, meditate, take a walk, and enjoy the smell of flowers.

I think it's an honorable and good thing to work hard. I truly do. And if someone is going to tip the balance scale one way or the other, I think it is probably good to let it go a little more to the work side than the play side (after all, there is that old saying about idle hands being the devil's workshop, which I totally believe to be true). But it's critical to have a little bit of down time and play time to enjoy life.

Something amazing happens when you step away from the craziness and just listen to the silence.

Something amazing happens when you step away from the craziness and just listen to the silence. You gain a perspective and a sense of calm that can help you make better decisions. You are able to see the full map of where you are going, appreciate the distance you have come, and realize how far you still need to go. You replenish your spirit.

Set goals for yourself on the time you will spend doing quality things with your family and the set goals for yourself on the time you will spend productively at work. And don't forget that you need to set a goal for the time you will spend just for you. Many of us (and I admit to being the worst at this) forget to set aside time just for ourselves. We get so busy taking care of everyone and everything around us that we forget about ourselves entirely. Take a little time to meditate each day by yourself. Clear your mind and just sit in silence. Somewhere beautiful and peaceful would be the best spot to do this, but anywhere quiet will work. Let your mind think about the beauty around you, think about your blessings, or think about nothing at all, and just be at peace. Then get up, take a deep breath, and enjoy the smell of flowers.

Learn to Say No So You'll Be Available to Say Yes When It Really Matters.

Saying no can be awkward, uncomfortable, and downright difficult. After all, it is human nature to want to be liked, and what better way to be liked than to make people happy by saying yes when they make a request of you? Not only do we want to be liked, but we want to avoid the feelings of guilt and/or shame that often accompany saying no to someone who we feel is showing their confidence in us by asking. Let's face it, it feels good to be needed, so the last thing we want is for people to stop needing us because we say no to them. And so we say yes far too often, to too many things, and we try to deal with all the stress and anxiety, and the subsequent health and mental issues that follow. But hey, at least we feel needed, right?!

I will fully admit that I have been sucked into that vortex of saying yes way too often in order to avoid ever having to say no to someone who needs me. And as a result, I have carried the stress and anxiety and all the other issues that come along with it until I finally reached the point that I began to recognize the insanity in saying yes to everything. They say the first step is recognizing your issue—check. They say the next step is admitting your issue—check. I don't know all of the steps in order, but I do know one of them is to figure out ways to rectify the problem, so I sat down and made a list of ways to help know when to say no.

- Set boundaries and stick with them. No exceptions. Early on in my career, I determined that I would never allow myself to work on Sunday. It was a set boundary that I never felt tempted to break, because I had made it a nonnegotiable for myself. Then when I recognized that I needed more dedicated family time, I added Saturday to that boundary as well. Everyone has to determine what their set boundaries will be in their own life, but whatever they are, I would advise that once you set them it is imperative that you never allow them to be broken. In my experience, if you allow yourself to break the boundaries even once, you will end up breaking that boundary again and again. Remember, it's only a true boundary if there are no exceptions.

- Just because you have an opening on your calendar doesn't mean you have to fill it. The reality is that there are plenty of things you need to get done that don't require a scheduled appointment, so consider those blank spaces on your calendar as invisible scheduled appointments for working on your to-do list.

- Don't answer immediately. In the moment, it's hard not to feel pressured into saying yes. Ask for time to look at your schedule so that you can step away and really think through if this is something you should take on or not.

- Ask yourself if saying yes is really the right thing to do. I used to encourage my employees to hang a sign in their cubicle stating "Is what I am doing right now leading me to accomplish my goal?" It served as a great tool for making

WHAT AWESOME LOOKS LIKE

people stop and consider if the activities that were filling their day were truly leading them to their end objective. Things come at us fast and furious, and we often get caught up doing "stuff" that isn't helping us progress toward our goals, so really consider whether taking this new assignment on will bring you closer to achieving your goals.

- You're not doing someone a favor if you say yes to something you don't have the capacity for. There are often things we would be willing to do, or feel obligated to do, or that we may even want to do, but before we say yes, we really need to check where the request would fall on our existing list of prioritized items. Once you've weighed it against the existing priorities, you have to be honest with yourself on whether this new request would be so far down the list that you realistically would not get to it in the time frame it needs to be done. Although your intent in saying yes might be to not let the person down, you could very well end up doing just that if you take something on that you truly don't have capacity to complete by the time they need it.

- Consider asking to modify the scope of what is being asked for. This is especially important when it comes to requests from clients or managers or board members. Often people ask you for something because they don't really understand the amount of time it would take to fulfill their request. A great example of this came up in a board meeting when one of the board members asked the management team to provide a report on a certain matter. The board member had no idea how complex that report would be to create, but the management team didn't feel comfortable saying no to a member of their board, so they agreed to do it. Luckily another board member spoke up and asked how much of management's time it would take to develop the report. When they explained the difficulty and time it would take, the first board member immediately withdrew the request and instead asked if there was a standard report that might shed light on the answers they were seeking. Remember, there is nothing wrong with expressing concern at how long something will take or asking if there are ways to modify an overwhelming request to make it more doable. Keep in mind that overly difficult requests usually stem from a lack of understanding that can easily be rectified with a little communication when it is done in a respectful way.

- Give people the right instruction when you are out of the office. It used to be that whenever I left town I almost felt obligated to bend over backwards with my out-of-office reply. I would apologetically state that I was out of the office but I would do everything I could to respond as quickly as possible, opening myself up to feeling obligated to check my emails and respond my entire vacation. So whose fault was that? Mine! Then one day I received an out-of-office reply from someone else that simply stated they would be away from email from this date to that date, with the direction that if I needed something I should recontact them once they had returned. With that simple reply, they had taken the burden off of their shoulders to respond and shifted it back to me to follow up with them once they were back. Genius!

Once you've considered the request against the items listed above, if the answer needs to be no, it is important to learn to say it in a respectful, yet direct fashion that doesn't require you to justify your answer or further explain yourself. You can always begin with a statement of appreciation such as "Thank you for thinking of me." Next, if it will help you feel better, you can add "I hate having to say no, but" followed by "I need to _____" or "I've got too much on my plate right now to be able to commit to that," or something along those lines. And finally, you can close by saying something to the effect of, "If circumstances change I will reach out and let you know," which clearly sends the message that they shouldn't keep checking with you, because you will be the one to contact them.

Saying no may never feel good, but I guarantee that being available to say yes when it really matters will.

CHAPTER 13

YOUR LIFE IS MEANT TO BE A MASTERPIECE

If Our Future Selves Could Talk to Us

It will all be okay in the end. If it's not okay, it's not the end.

—Unknown

I lived in Virginia for part of my teenage years. During a recent visit to the White House in Washington, DC, I was able to drive past the house I'd lived in nearly thirty years before. Driving up, a million memories flooded my mind as if they'd happened just yesterday. As I looked up at the second story window to what used to be my bedroom, I could picture myself hanging out in my room listening to my eighties music cassette tapes while cutting out pictures from fashion magazines to hang on my walls.

I couldn't help but think, "If only that teenage girl knew all the things she would face in her life … all the struggles she would go through … the heartaches she would experience … the fears she would face … the years of loneliness and struggles she'd have as a single mom … the businesses she would build … the ups and the downs she would have to get through … the burdens she would shoulder … the lessons she would learn … the two beautiful children she would be blessed with who would grow up to become the most amazing adults … the perfect little grandson who would come into her life and become the sun, moon, and stars … the losses she would suffer … the success she would have … the tears she would shed … the amazing friendships she'd form … the incredible people she would get to interact with … the happiness she would feel … the countless blessings that would be bestowed upon her …"

I'm certain if that teenage girl had been told what lay in store for her in the next thirty years of her life she would never have been able to believe it. She would never have thought she could be strong enough to get through all the hard times ahead. She would never have believed she was capable of standing strong through such heavy trials. She would never have thought she was smart enough to achieve all the successes in business.

We are *all* so much stronger, more capable, and smarter than we have even begun to realize. Whatever age we are today, I believe that if our future selves could talk to us right now, they would say, "Know that there are challenges ahead that won't be easy, but know that getting through them

We are *all* so much stronger, more capable, and smarter than we have even begun to realize.

will be worth it … and you *are* going to get through them … *all* of them … and you are going to be better for it."

Diagnosis: Entrepreneurs Disease

Entrepreneurs are all in, all the time. Entrepreneurs love what they do and obsess over it. It is a predisposition; a path that has already been laid for you. It is a character trait, a labor of love, a zeal that cannot be trained, a condition that cannot be treated, an illness that cannot be caught. You've either got it or you don't.

—Jeff Stibel

I had successfully built a company and sold it for $377 million. I had completed a six-month transition period after the sale, and it was supposed to be my first official day of never having to work another day in my life if I didn't want to. But I couldn't stop myself.

Why? I had Entrepreneurs Disease, and there was just no denying it.

For the last sixteen years, I had woken up every morning and rushed out the door without time for breakfast, always at least ten minutes late for my first meeting of the day and praying for a Diet Coke to magically appear on my desk to get me through. I spent my days in back-to-back meetings with executives and employees, on conference calls with clients, reviewing contracts, designing software, coming up with new branding and marketing strategies, heading back into meetings, answering more phone calls, wading through endless emails (that I could never actually get through), and then getting out the door when it was way past dark to head home and spend an hour writing my nightly blog to my employees before finally climbing into bed, only to wake up five hours later and do it all again. Oh, and I forgot to mention that most nights my dreams were full of to-do lists and new brilliant business ideas that I hoped in my sleep to remember the next day, but usually didn't.

For sixteen long years I had done that. For sixteen long years I thought to myself, *What would it be like to have my life back? What would it be like to have a calendar that wasn't packed full of appointments, or an email box that I could actually get through? I bet that would be glorious!*

Yet here it was, my first day of retirement—I jumped out of bed thinking, *There is so much to do! There is a website to build, business cards to finish, a new office space to build out, new furniture to order, insurance to set up, contract templates to create, and meetings to attend.* I worked my behind off all day, finally sitting down to write my daily blog at nine o'clock at night. That's when it hit me—I AM SERIOUSLY SICK—I've got Entrepreneurs Disease!

I don't know how to wake up and not hit the ground running. I don't know how to have nothing to do. And there is not a doggone thing that I can do about it; it's in my DNA, so really I blame my father, who couldn't waste a day if his life depended on it. I am doomed to a life full of hardworking days and lofty goals that, once accomplished, simply grow larger and harder to achieve, because I am, and always will be, an entrepreneur.

So how do I feel about having this disease? I have come to accept it and embrace it, because that is who I am. And I've come to appreciate that my disease is FANTASTIC! Why? Because I love having an endless list of goals to achieve; I love the challenge of seeing a problem and knowing I can create a solution for it; I love the excitement that comes from

I am doomed to a life full of hardworking days and lofty goals that, once accomplished, simply grow larger and harder to achieve.

building something from the ground up; I love the thought of taking a vision and making it a reality; I love the ability to surround myself with a great team; I love the feeling I get when I can climb into bed at night knowing that I achieved as much as humanly possible that day without wasting a moment of this glorious life God gave me.

Yes, I LOVE being an entrepreneur—no treatment necessary!

Life After Selling a Business

As an entrepreneur, you start a business with the goal of someday selling it and getting a big payoff. You devote your entire life to making it a success, working your guts out, putting in crazy hours, and making many sacrifices to grow your company. Then one day that payoff finally comes, and you suddenly realize you have no idea what the heck is supposed to come next. At least that was my experience.

Going Through the Sale of a Company

The process of selling the company became all-consuming. All of my time was spent in due diligence and negotiations, not to mention the endless review of legal documents needed for the closing. Through all of that, I was determined not to let my mind think past the closing itself. I didn't want to allow myself to get emotionally attached to having the deal close, as I knew that would weaken my ability to negotiate the best terms. Especially where I had seen other entrepreneurs become so excited about life after the sale that the closer they came to having their deals close, the less objective they were in the negotiations, and in their eagerness they became willing to give away too much.

While this strategy helped me tremendously in keeping a level head throughout the acquisition, the one area it hurt me was in my emotional preparedness for life after the closing. I knew that the day I signed the closing papers it would no longer be my company, and I knew that everything I had built for so many years was now going to belong to someone else. I knew all of that in my head, but I don't know if I was prepared for it in my heart. I suppose most entrepreneurs aren't prepared for the emotions they will experience as they sell their business, because it's hard to comprehend exactly how it will feel until you actually go through it. However, I will try to put into words how it felt for me, in the hopes of helping the next person who will walk this same path.

Letting Your Baby Grow Up and Move On

What did it feel like to sell the company? There is a sense of excitement and accomplishment for achieving your ultimate goal as an entrepreneur. At the same time, there is a sense of sadness and loss.

The closest comparison I can think of would be the feeling of sending a child off to college for the first time. Similar to raising a child, you put your heart and soul into preparing the company to go on without you and succeed on its own. You just hope and pray that you have done enough to prepare the team to be okay on their own. There is no question that it is a very unsettling feeling, but deep down you have to trust that you have done everything you can for them, and know they will grow even more once they don't have you to rely on anymore. Then you pray you have left a positive legacy of leadership behind.

Dealing with Your Own Identity

I had been the CEO of my own business for so long that once we sold, it was definitely disconcerting to realize that I had to figure out who I was now that it wasn't my business any longer. In the months following the sale, during the transition period, I began to ponder what I wanted my future to be. There was no denying that it feels different to know that you are building a business for someone else rather than for your own team. And let's be honest—entrepreneurs by nature are people who have been willing to bank their entire lives on themselves. They are willing to take risks that depend on THEM, because deep down they trust themselves, and therefore they don't see it as risky. But entrepreneurs are not comfortable letting someone else take the reins, which is why they start and run their own companies in the first place. As I came to recognize how I was feeling about things, I decided it was time for me to step out and once again bet on myself. This time, I wanted to bet on myself doing something I had always dreamed of. After all, what was the point of working so hard for a payout if I wasn't going to use that freedom to pursue something I had always dreamed of doing?

Why Not Retire?

I woke up the day after leaving my company at six-thirty in the morning, and I hit the ground running in order to launch my next venture. When you have pushed yourself for years and years, it becomes an absolute habit and part of your very makeup. And suddenly, when you no longer have to do it, there's a massive increase—not decrease—in your energy level, because now you are able to focus on all the things you are excited to work on. Nothing is more energizing than that—it's the best adrenaline rush there is!

What was the point of working so hard for a payout if I wasn't going to use that freedom to pursue something I had always dreamed of doing?

And frankly I didn't know how to stand still. It's in my blood. There's no point fighting it, so I may as well embrace it and move forward with accomplishing the next seemingly insurmountable goal in my life, because that is what entrepreneurs do!

Balancing "Want to Dos" with What Matters Most

For the first time in my life, it's no longer a list of "have to dos," it's a list of "want to dos." But deciding which "want to do" gets to come first can be a struggle. Patience has never been my best virtue, which helped me be a good entrepreneur but made me a terrible prioritizer.

In my mind, everything is Priority Number One. Everything needs to get done yesterday. I tend to set ridiculously short timelines on projects for myself in order to get as many things done as possible. Is it wrong to do that? I don't know. It certainly helped me to be successful in my professional life. At the same time, it comes at a price—which is why it's important to take the time to slow down in order to focus on what truly matters most—in my case, my husband, my children, my grandchildren, my parents, and my extended family. When this life is over, no matter what amazing things I've accomplished, not one of them will ever have as much meaning to me as my accomplishments with my own family

Starting the Next Chapter of Life

I had always dreamed of taking everything I have learned—my failures, my successes, the leadership principles, and the strategies that ultimately led to my success—and sharing them, in hopes of helping others excel faster and easier than I did. What better way to make our trials in life count for something positive than by using them to help others? It was that desire to help others to excel that led me to launch REES Capital (www.rees-capital.com), my angel investing firm, and the IPOP Foundation (www.ipop.org), which stands for "In Pursuit Of Perfection,"

> I had always dreamed of taking everything I have learned—my failures, my successes, the leadership principles, and the strategies that ultimately led to my success—and sharing them, in hopes of helping others excel faster and easier than I did.

and is a charity focused on helping promote, educate, and perpetuate entrepreneurship as a pathway to self-reliance, and it's what drives me to continue writing my daily blogs (www.amyreesanderson.com/blog).

Yes, there is life after selling your business, and for an entrepreneur, it is a life filled with even larger and more meaningful goals yet to be accomplished, because we simply are not satisfied to think small.

There is no passion to be found playing small—in settling for a life that is less than the one you are capable of living.

—Nelson Mandela

Don't Limit the Picture in Your Mind

Don't limit the picture in your mind because God intends your picture to be a masterpiece.

—Amy Rees Anderson

The greatest lesson that my journey thus far has taught me is to never limit the picture we have in our minds, because God intends that picture to be a masterpiece.

I didn't start out thinking I'd be a successful businessperson. I was just a twenty-three-year-old girl who'd dropped out of college, trying to raise two little children alone, and needing a way to put food on the table. But I'm so glad I chose to become an entrepreneur. Sure, it has been an incredibly challenging lifestyle—balance is a constant struggle—but I have learned more amazing lessons through trying and failing and trying and failing, and continuing to get back up to keep moving forward, than I could have learned any other way.

For those considering entrepreneurship as their career, I would say this: You will have to work your guts out more than anyone could ever prepare you for. You will take more bumps and bruises and more scrapes and cuts than there are Band-Aids to cover. Your failures will be seen by many and your efforts will often be appreciated by few. But at the end of the day, I can't think of any other career that will force you to learn and grow at such an unbelievable pace and allow you the chance to influence other people's lives by affording them opportunities to excel—all while giving you the canvas to create something truly spectacular. Yes, I'm glad I chose to be an entrepreneur, and I wouldn't change it for the world.

Entrepreneurship is living a few years of your life like most people won't, so you can spend the rest of your life like most people can't.

—Unknown

As I've said before, the greatest successes in life don't always require the mind of a genius or huge sums of money. The greatest successes are often achieved by very ordinary people who make a very extraordinary effort. So I challenge you to go make your own Goal Poster, and when you do, don't hold back. Go big ... GO REALLY BIG! And whatever you do, don't limit that picture in your mind, or on your poster, because I promise you that what God intends is for your picture to be a masterpiece.

Then get up, do something, do anything ... just make a start.

Because YOU are what AWESOME looks like!

USE YOUR VOICE TO LEAVE A LEGACY

Since 2010, I've been writing a daily blog every day, five days a week. I am proud to say that with the exception of national holidays, I've never missed a day. It's been one of my great accomplishments to achieve the goal of never missing a day, and that blog has turned into a journal of the amazing things I've learned.

The subject of each blog typically stems from something I went through or experienced during that particular day that then stuck in my mind as I sat down that evening to write. At times, I share lessons I learned as an entrepreneur and CEO; other times, I share lessons that stem from my experiences as an angel investor. Most days, I share thoughts and lessons I'm learning about life in general. I write it in hope that all I learn will extend beyond myself and help others to excel.

I also do it in the hope that one day, many years from now when I am no longer on this earth, my great, great grandchildren can know who I was, all that I believed, and what values I stood for. And may I have lived my life in such a way that I've left a legacy they will be proud of.

WWW.AMYREESANDERSON.COM/BLOG

BOOKS THAT HAVE HELPED ME EXCEL

Seek ye out of the best books words of wisdom.

—*Doctrine and Covenants 88:118*

I'd like to share some of the books that helped me most in my role as a CEO and a leader:

Who Moved My Cheese? by Spencer Johnson, MD

This is one of my favorite books in life, and here's why: (1) It's easy to read because it has big print—and pictures, too! (2) It's about two mice and two men, and who doesn't love a story about mice? (3) It has one of the best messages about letting go of the past, getting over the things you cannot change, moving forward, and realizing there is no reason to fear the unknown because the unknown may be better than anything you could have imagined. With effortless simplicity, this little book teaches that things in life don't always go as expected, and when that happens we have two choices: we can curl up and die, or we can go find new cheese. This book will inspire you to overcome your fears of the unknown and to recognize the need to venture into new territory so that you can find all the blessings that life has in store for you. Anyone who is facing a challenge, a loss, or a disappointment in life will find this book to be a true lifesaver. It's definitely a must read.

The Four Obsessions of an Extraordinary Executive: A Leadership Fable by Patrick Lencioni

This book taught me a tremendous amount about how great leaders take responsibility for creating and perpetuating the culture of their company. It truly shaped my views on the importance of (1) selecting a great executive team, (2) creating a clear direction with easy-to-understand measurements of success for the company, (3) overcommunicating to your company every single day, and (4) reinforcing the culture of the company by hiring and supporting a fantastic team of people who embrace the culture and desire to make it succeed.

Feel the Fear … and Do It Anyway by Susan Jeffers, PhD

I discussed why I love this book already. It's all about feeling fear but not letting it stop you from doing the things you really want to do in life.

Confronting the Myth of Self-Esteem: Twelve Keys to Finding Peace by Ester Rasband

The title of this book may make some wonder what this has to do with being a CEO and a leader, but there is not one of us who hasn't struggled with self-esteem at one point or another. A simple Google search on the term "self-esteem" elicits over one hundred and forty million results. Clearly this is a subject that many struggle with. Some might assume that a person in leadership wouldn't have self-esteem issues. After all, they are the leader. But that is like assuming every supermodel believes she is beautiful. News story after news story of eating disorders, drug use, and suicide attempts among models would show that not to be true. Self-esteem, or the search for it, is something that touches all of our lives at some point. It touched my life in my late twenties. I had gone through a divorce and was struggling. As I walked through a bookstore, a few words in the title of this book caught my attention—"the myth of self-esteem." How could it refer to self-esteem as a myth when it was the search for it that was impacting my own life so greatly? As I devoured its pages, this book taught me that feeling good about oneself will never be found by seeking it from external sources—it will only be found by the act of doing good. It also taught me that inner peace comes from giving our best efforts in selfless service of others. Ultimately, this book taught me that true self-esteem doesn't come from the opinions and praise of others, but from having a knowledge of who we truly are, which we find when we build a relationship with God, the universe, or whatever higher power we personally believe in. This book was genuinely life changing, and I wouldn't be the person I am today without having read it.

The Seven Spiritual Laws of Success: A Practical Guide to the Fulfillment of Your Dreams by Deepak Chopra

This book touched me spiritually, helping me to look inward for answers. It points out the fear-based ways of thinking that hold us back, encourages looking for comfort in the uncertainty of life rather than attempting to control that which cannot be controlled, and explains that what we focus on each day is what our future will hold. This book helped me understand that the best way to find success in my own life is to help others achieve success in theirs. That lesson alone became a driving principle in all I did in business, and ultimately I believe it was living that principle that had the greatest impact on the amazing success we achieved.

The Book of Mormon, Another Testament of Jesus Christ

I can emphatically say that this book, along with the Bible, has been the absolute key to my success—both in life and in business. This book taught me what being a great leader looks like. It taught me every value I strive to uphold. It taught me why I need to get back up each time I fall down. It taught me to believe in something bigger than myself. Without having read this book, I can honestly say that I wouldn't be the person I am today and that I would not have accomplished what I've been able to accomplish. If I were to recommend the most important book I've ever read, this would be it.

———

We have a finite number of hours in our day, and what we do with those hours will make all the difference to our future success. Make time to read great books that can teach you important life lessons.

Don't waste precious minutes on meaningless activities that don't contribute to making you a better person. When you wake up in the morning, have inspirational books and talks playing while you get ready for the day. When you commute to and from work, listen to motivational books and talks along the way. Find pockets of time to let the great life lessons of others lift you, teach you, and shape you into the very best that you can become.

ACKNOWLEDGEMENTS

It's been said that it takes a village, and I can tell you that my life wouldn't be all that it's been without the awesome people who have been part of my village. My grandparents, my parents, my siblings, my children, my grandchild(ren), my mentors, my advisors, my past employees, my friends, and the most important person in my life and very best friend—my husband. I could not have achieved the success that I have without their examples, their love, and their support. THEY are what AWESOME looks like!

ABOUT THE AUTHOR

Amy Rees Anderson is the founder and managing partner of REES Capital, an angel investing firm. Amy is also an author of a daily blog and is a contributor to *Forbes* and the Huffington Post. She is an in-demand public speaker, a respected mentor, and she lectures at a number of universities.

Prior to founding REES Capital, Amy Rees Anderson was formerly the founder and CEO of MediConnect Global, Inc., one of the largest cloud-based health information exchanges. In March 2012, Amy successfully led MediConnect to being acquired for over $377 million.

After selling MediConnect, she founded the IPOP Foundation (In Pursuit of Perfection), a charity focused on helping promote, educate, and perpetuate entrepreneurship as a pathway to self-reliance.

Amy has been the recipient of a number of awards, which include receiving the prestigious Ernst & Young Entrepreneur of the Year Award and being named CEO of the Year. She has been featured on the cover of *Inc.*, in the *Wall Street Journal*, *Businessweek*, and many other national publications as a result of her many accomplishments. In 2015, Amy received an honorary PhD.

Amy is married to Rollin Anderson, has two married children, and one adorable grandchild. Amy and her husband reside in Utah.

BOOK AMY TO SPEAK

Book Amy Rees Anderson to speak for your company, conference, university, or event!

Amy Rees Anderson is an in-demand public speaker. Through her contagious enthusiasm, Amy creates a sense of urgency that leaves audiences with a passion to get up and do something that will move them forward toward reaching their ultimate goals for life. Amy is also a frequent lecturer on college campuses around the country and never fails to be an audience favorite.

To book Amy to speak, go to www.amyreesanderson.com/contact and submit a request for speaking along with the information that you are looking for.

Follow Amy's daily blog at www.amyreesanderson.com/blog.

LINKEDIN	linkedin.com/in/amyreesanderson
TWITTER	@amyreesanderson.com
FACEBOOK	https://www.facebook.com/amyreesanderson

Create your goal poster and share an image of it with Amy on social media by tagging @amyreesanderson and adding the hashtag #goalposter